AR2

HANDBOOK FOR THE SECOND

AMERICAN REVOLUTION

LAWRENCE PAUL HEBRON

ISBN: 1492751537

ISBN-13: 9781492751533

Library of Congress Control Number: 2013917138

CreateSpace Independent Publishing Platform

North Charleston, South Carolina

THIS BOOK IS DEDICATED TO

GOD AND THE UNITED STATES OF AMERICA

WITH SPECIAL APPRECIATION TO

Walter   Ena

Dori

Lisa   Heather

Keith   Ryan

and heartfelt affection for the First Rebels of the
Second Revolution

Carl B., Robert N., Mary N., Scott N., Laura C., Gwen Y.,
Tony B., Nancy G., Mike R., Jeane R., James Y., Gary D.,
Steve E., Yvonne E., John F., Pat L., John M., Terry M.,
Dorothy G., Charles D.

Grateful thanks to my editor, Leah Freeman, who made this a better book. It has been said that the goal of great teachers is to become dispensable to their students. Perhaps an even greater honor is ultimately to be taught by them. You must have had some fine teachers, for now you have grown to teach them.

Grateful thanks to Christopher Pradzinski for applying his considerable talents to bring the Revolution to life through his graphic artistry.

TABLE OF CONTENTS

PART ONE

THE COURSE OF HUMAN EVENTS

CHAPTER ONE

TELLERS AND LETTERS

Memorial Day weekend. As I talked with a few friends before the beginning of the Sunday morning worship service, I noticed Chuck slowly making his way into the sanctuary. He used a walker most of the time now. His aging body disguised the virile and vital life he had lived. On this day, however, my thoughts ran to but one aspect of that life. I broke off my conversation with the others and walked over to Chuck. We greeted each other and shook hands. Both his greeting and his handshake remained vigorous. "Chuck, I want to thank you for your service."

Chuck is a veteran of World War II. I wanted him to know that his sacrifice was remembered and appreciated. I didn't expect the reaction I received. His eyes dropped to the floor. His head bowed and then began to drift slowly back and forth. He finally spoke. "It's not like it used to be." I said nothing. The old warrior was experiencing something – processing something – and I felt

3

it was best to remain silent. He continued. "The country has changed – and not for the better." There was another pause, and then he looked up at me. His old eyes had glazed over with tears. "This isn't what I fought for."

His words stabbed at my heart. Suddenly Chuck's demeanor seemed to be an allegory for all of America. The once vital and virile warrior – a crusader for the cause of liberty – appeared lost and defeated. Not by age, but by betrayal. Our beloved America had been betrayed. The ideal worth dying for had itself died.

Or, had it? Wracked by woes, overshadowed by affliction, and definitely on the decline, it would be easy to consign the United States to the ash heap of history. Were it any other nation, that prediction would undoubtedly prove correct. But this is not any other nation. This is the United States of America. We have proved time and time again that we are made of a coarse grit that is not so easily ground into powder. Our evolution is revolution. We were born in blood and have proved over and over that we will shed that blood as profusely as needed in order to stand resolutely for the cause of right.

But, what is "right?" Politicians representing every hue across the political spectrum are busy telling us that they are right. Still, someone must be wrong – maybe nearly everyone. Have you noticed? No matter which party we elect, things get worse. If one of them is right, then how come things keep going wrong? Could it be that we have fallen into some parallel political universe where nothing works? Or, could it be that we have slipped away from that new universe which we forged in 1776 and have fallen back into the old ways of serfdom that had been the norm for ages upon ages?

Historians and philosophers have nimble and polished methods for making simple things look complicated. Perhaps it is because they themselves do not understand what they are describing; perhaps they don't want us to understand what they are up to; or perhaps it is just their way of creating job security. Regardless, at the junction of history and philosophy there is a profound simplicity which has been virtually ignored by those who study both. Here it is. There are basically two types of people: "*Tellers*" and "*Letters*." Each group makes fundamentally different assumptions about people and life. These assumptions, in turn, result in fundamentally different operating styles when *dealing* with people and life. The *Tellers* and *Letters* tend to project these assumptions into every aspect of their existence. They conjure radically different ideologies, and they create radically different realities, which the students of philosophy and history must then chronicle. *Tellers* assume that they are entitled to impose their will on others – by virtue of their superior intelligence, wisdom, experience, or because they simply have the power to do so and are not overly burdened by a conscience. They seek to "tell" others what to do. *Letters* may or may not believe that they possess superior intellect or wisdom or experience, but they do not presume that they are entitled to impose their will on others. They believe they should "let" people live their own lives – even if they don't make the best decisions – unless those decisions hurt others. *Tellers* are the less mature and more tyrannical of the two types. *Letters* are the more mature and less despotic of the two. Without question, the *Tellers* tend to dominate both in history and in personal relations. There are simply a lot of tyrants in the world – both petty and grand.

Those who peruse the annals of history get to study little else but *Tellers*. Typically, some confluence of circumstances deposits a considerable amount of power in the hands of a person or small group of people who then shamefully use that power to pursue their own selfish interests by telling others what to do. A small group prevails while the masses wail.

In more recent centuries, the oppression has cloaked itself with a philosophical air. Apparently, the *Tellers* have come to feel the need to adorn themselves in some form of philosophical justification other than bald self interest. One such justification which has played a dominant role in the last two centuries has been Marxism. Marx sought to distribute economic wealth among all who participated in creating it (the proletariat), as opposed to concentrating it among those who organized its production (the bourgeoisie). At first glance his ideology sounds noble and fair, which is why it lives on despite an almost unparalleled record of failure. The trouble with Marxism, and other types of socialism, is that it is founded upon colossally erroneous assumptions about human nature. Marxists actually believe that laborers will perpetually work their tails off and then willingly, happily, surrender the fruits of their labor so some bureaucrat can decide who deserves it. The problem with "From each according to his ability; to each according to his need" (the mantra of Marxism) is that it separates hard work from the payoff for hard work; and people simply won't do that for very long – unless they are forced to. And this is where the *Tellers* go to work under Marxism. In order for the system to function at all, the overseers must continually strive to pound the square pegs of human nature into the round holes of philosophical assumptions. It gets to be pretty painful it you happen to be one of the pegs; and, make no mistake about it, the pegs are comprised of both the bourgeoisie and the proletariat.

In the latter part of the nineteenth century, another philosophical movement emerged called "Progressivism." (Oh my, modern-day *Tellers* have a special gift for marketing and euphemisms.) In reality, the Progressives are kissing cousins (or is that salacious siblings) of the Marxists. A key tenant of the Progressive philosophy is the belief that society should be managed by experts. Again, like the Marxist tagline, this sounds like a wonderful and remarkably rational idea. After all, you wouldn't want to trust your upcoming double bypass operation to some eighth grade dropout, would you? Unfortunately, and euphony notwithstanding, the practical operating assumption of Progressivism boils down to this: the masses are simply too darn stupid to know how to run their own lives, so we will do it for them. Once again, we have the

Tellers forcing the square pegs into the round holes. And so we get government-managed pensions, government-managed heath care, government-managed schools, government-managed economy, government-managed banks, government-managed job creation; and, of course, the government-managed catastrophe that goes along with it all. This catastrophe is largely the work of the Progressive *Tellers* who have had a prevailing influence over the course of the political, economic, and social "progress" of America for well over a century.

The bulk of history has been dominated by *Tellers*. Accordingly, the cumulative miseries of mankind largely have been perpetrated by the *Tellers*. However, there was an exception – a bright and shining moment in history when the *Letters* held sway. It started within a string of colonies hugging the east coast of North America. Its conception took place in the early seventeenth century. Its gestation proceeded into the late-mid eighteenth century. Its birth certificate was called a Declaration of Independence. This Declaration was the voice of *Letters* crying in the wilderness. That voice had been heard before, but this time it rang out with a fury that would not be ignored and could not be stopped.

The relationship between the Colonies and the royal government of Great Britain had always been prickly, but after the conclusion of the French and Indian War, that relationship hit the skids and cascaded toward catastrophe. The war had been extremely costly for Great Britain, and the home government sought to have the colonists help bear the burden. The Stamp Act of 1765 and the Townshend Act of 1767 were examples of Parliament's policy of having the colonies pay their "fair share" of the costs for maintaining the Empire. Colonial protests resulted in the repeal of both acts, but Parliament clung to its right to legislate for the colonies in the Declaratory Act of 1766. The abusive regulations continued. In 1773 Parliament passed the Tea Act which restricted commerce and imposed a costly duty on this popular beverage. When the protest of the locals went unheeded, a band of rebels, many disguised as Indians, boarded British ships in Boston Harbor on the night of December 16, 1773, and threw their cargo overboard. Protesters in three other colonies also responded and prevented the unloading of the taxed tea in their harbors as well. The revolt was spreading. Parliament reacted in 1774 with the passage of the Coercive Acts or, as they were known in the Colonies, the Intolerable Acts. Among other things, these laws stripped the rebellious colony of Massachusetts of its power of self-government as well as other historic rights. Americans up and down the seaboard could see the handwriting on the wall. It wasn't hard to imagine where this was headed, and many responded with outrage. The fuse had been lit. It was only a matter of time until the "shot heard 'round the world" would propel the Colonies into open and violent rebellion.

On July 4, 1776, the Second Continental Congress approved a statement which proclaimed "That these United Colonies are, and of Right ought to be Free and

Independent States...." The document was a masterpiece. Among other things it delineated the proper role of government and explained why "these United Colonies" were morally and legally entitled to "dissolve the political bands" which had bound them to Great Britain and to establish "Free and Independent States." In short, the parent government had rendered itself illegitimate when it violated its most sacred trust and purpose. It had consistently abused the "unalienable Rights" which the "Creator" had "endowed" to "all men." The protection of those rights is why "Governments are instituted among Men." Furthermore, "whenever any Form of Government becomes destructive of these ends, it is the Right of the People to alter or abolish it, and to institute new Government...."

The Declaration approved on July 4, 1776, was a broadside fired by the *Letters* against the *Tellers*. It affirmed the God-given rights of the people to be allowed – *let* – to live their lives the way they saw fit as long as they did not deny someone else the same rights. The rebels proclaimed that they intended to live as free men and would no longer grovel under the whip of the *Tellers*. From Lexington to Yorktown they proved their resolve – their only options were liberty or death. In the end, the *Tellers* slunk back into the shadows. A new age had dawned – the Age of the *Letters*.

The real revolution of 1776 was not about bullets and bombs nor armies and navies. The *real* revolution was about a simple idea that boiled down to this: we will create a society and a government that will *let* you live your life as you see fit as long as you *let* others do likewise. It was simple. It was radical. It was almost unheard of. It worked. That string of colonies hugging the east coast of North America became history's grandest and noblest superpower. This is no jingoistic claim. It is a rock-hard fact confirmed by the millions of people who came here from every corner of the world in order to share in the glory of America. They came for a chance. They came to live freely as *Letters* instead of living under the oppression of *Tellers*. They made history.

But History has an inertia of its own – an energy that is fueled by the dark nature of humankind. The sad fact is that the *Tellers* far outnumber the *Letters*. The dynamic of History will always be inclined to devolve into a system where *Tellers* prevail, and they are driven by the mighty engine of the morally immature: selfishness.

Although most people are inclined to be *Tellers*, most of them do not have what it takes to rise to the level of the Master *Tellers*. The masses – the Petty *Tellers* – are not smart enough to become successful manipulators. They are destined to become the manipulated. If only they were a little smarter they would realize that *all Tellers* are driven by selfish ambitions, but that only the Master *Tellers* will prevail; and when they do, they will impose their selfish ambitions on all, but only the Masters will benefit. If only the masses of Petty *Tellers* were a little smarter they would realize that the system of the *Letters* is their best bet. But, they are not that smart; and so they readily fall prey to the manipulations and machinations of Master *Tellers* who are smarter than they are and who enslave them by playing on their dim wits and selfish tendencies. The Master *Tellers* promise all manner of selfish blessings to the Petty *Tellers*: better pay, guaranteed pensions, universal healthcare, easy loans, quick divorce, fast bankruptcy, free this, and carefree that. Poor simpletons. They cannot see that it is merely bait in the trap. It is the ploy of the Master *Tellers* to get them to trade freedom for security while achieving neither. The only winners are a relative handful of Master *Tellers* who play the game better than others. And what do these *Tellers* win? They become powerful. They become our masters. They get to tell us how to live our lives, and we must let them. This is the New America. It is the America of the *Tellers*. It is a betrayal of our founding ideas, of our uniqueness, of our greatness, of our past, and of our future. This is not the America that Chuck fought for.

America is definitely ill, but whether this illness will prove mortal is yet to be determined. It all boils down to this: if we are still Americans, then we will overcome and prevail. But, if we have become merely people who live in America, then all is lost. So, who are we? Who are you? Are you an American, or do you simply live here? To find the answer to that question, you will have to search your own heart and soul. If you are stirred to fight back, sacrifice, and – if need be – die for the cause of 1776, then arise. You are an American, and your country needs you again. If you are not stirred to fight, sacrifice, and possibly die, then you are just living here. You are not American, and you need to get out of the way of those who are. We have a job to do. And, by God, we will do it.

*   *   *

The document approved by the Second Continental Congress on July 4, 1776, was more than just a Declaration of Independence. It was a proclamation of the rightful role of government. It was a justification for rebellion against illegitimate authority. It was a declaration of war.

So is this document.

In a tragic case of historical irony, the very institution which was established to fight an illegitimate government has become one. The very government which was established to defend God-given, unalienable rights has chosen to deny God and alienate these rights from its people. And the very document, the Declaration of Independence, which was drafted to justify the establishment of this independent government will now judge that same government. The verdict is "guilty." The sentence? "[W]henever any Form of Government becomes destructive of these ends, it is the Right of the People to alter or abolish it, and to institute new Government...."

The political reality in modern-day America can be succinctly stated with these few words:

The government is corrupt.
The political system is dysfunctional.

Both political parties have not only failed us, they have betrayed us.

We cannot trust them with our future.

We must take back control ourselves.

Everything is at stake.

The time has come for "we the people" to rise up and claim what is rightfully ours.

The time has come to mutually pledge to each other our lives, our fortunes, and our sacred honor.

The time has come for the Second American Revolution.

This is what we fight for.

AR2.

CHAPTER TWO

THREE LAWS OF POLITICAL HISTORY.

Some laws are written on paper by the hand of man. Some are not. The laws of man are often fickle, mercurial, and ephemeral. The paper upon which they are inscribed will likely last longer than they will. But then, there is the other class of laws. These are etched with iron into stone and woven into the very fabric of life. They are immutable and inescapable; any human legislator would be well advised to know and honor them. To ignore them is to position oneself in the path of the avalanche, for your petty scribblings will ultimately, and likely soon, be crushed by them. Of these, three are especially relevant to our current purposes. We *must* understand these if we are to have any hope of rebuilding America the Great.

The First Law of Political History: *Throughout the centuries, across the continents, among all cultures, a small*

15

minority has always sought to exploit the power of the state in order to oppress and plunder the productive majority.

"Government" has consistently proved to be the favorite tool of tyrants and criminals – both petty and grand alike – in pursuing their egomaniacal objectives. The consequence has always been inevitable. The greatest abuser of personal liberties has always been government. The greatest tool of organized criminals has always been government. The greatest mass-murderer throughout the ages has always been government. It is one of the most powerful and persistent themes of history: a small minority has always sought – and will always seek – to exploit the power of the state in order to oppress and plunder the productive majority. Call it what you will – monarchy, oligarchy, tyranny, democracy – it has almost always proved to work that way. Almost. There have been few and rare exceptions, the greatest of which occurred on the eastern coast of North America in the 1770s. An exceptional assemblage of philosopher farmers and patriots placed their trust in the protection of divine Providence and pledged their lives, their fortunes, and their sacred honor to fight for the cause of liberty by fighting against the oppression of big government. For many, it cost their lives and their fortunes, but never their honor. Their names are inscribed in Heaven and on Earth as protectors of the noblest of causes and as defenders of personal rights. Humankind is forever in their debt, and God has surely welcomed them home with the cherished greeting, "Well done, good and faithful servant."

The Second Law of Political History. *Power will always tend to be abused. The only way to prevent this abuse is to prevent the accumulation of great power – anywhere.*

With the exception of a few utopian philosophers, most of the astute observers of humanity have felt compelled to address the dark side of our nature. Whether we are "fallen" or never even rose high enough to fall, it is apparent to most students of the human condition that we are inclined to be bottom dwellers in the morass of immorality. Of course there have been bright flashes of virtue throughout our history, but they have been comparatively rare, short-lived, and have resulted from the compelling force of an inspired personality. When that personality passes, the light dims and, frequently, goes out all together. Given the reality of our wicked inclinations, it should be obvious that we need to do two things: (1) plan to minimize the harmful consequences that will derive from this shameful nature of ours and (2) take action to change that nature. At present, we are doing neither.

(1) We cannot plan to minimize the harmful consequences which derive from our sinful nature unless we first recognize its root cause: selfishness. Think about it. Virtually everything which is called a "sin" (from a theological perspective) or a "crime" (from a secular, legalist point of view) originates with a selfish motive that works to the detriment of another person. Selfishness is the sinister seed of corruption, but by itself it can accomplish little. It needs a collaborator – a co-conspirator – to give it wings, and that collaborator is power.

He is remembered for little else, but Lord John Emerich Edward Dalberg-Acton gave us an insightful – though inaccurate – maxim that we would do well to consider here. "All power tends to corrupt, and absolute power corrupts absolutely." The remark is inaccurate because power does not corrupt. We already are corrupt. Even the most powerless of us – the infirm, incapacitated, and decrepit – are corrupt. They are simply in no position to act on their desires. The remark is insightful because it speaks to the necessary connecting link between our corrupt inclinations and our corrupt behavior: power.

Rightly speaking, power does not corrupt. It gives vent. It allows our inner desires to be externalized and realized. If we are good by nature, power enables us to do good things. If we are bad by nature, power enables us to do bad things. For most of humanity, this second outcome is the more likely prospect. Few of us ever rise very far above our selfish interests. Accordingly, the acquisition of power will simply allow those who acquire this power to pursue their selfish interests more successfully. Almost invariably this will work to the detriment of others – which we said is the defining characteristic of both sin and crime. Here we see the connection between power and corruption. Power enables our selfish nature to express itself, thereby resulting in corrupt behavior.

So, how do we minimize the potential for corruption? Simple. Limit the amount of power that any person or group of persons can amass and utilize. This applies to all kinds of power: political, economic, religious, etc.

Since we can pretty well count on the fact that any kind of power will be misused (that is, used for the selfish benefit of those who have the power and used to the detriment of those who do not have the power), permitting the accumulation and concentration of power anywhere is profoundly dangerous and foolhardy. It is a game only played by simpletons and scoundrels.

Nowhere has this tendency toward abuse been more evident than in the political history of governments. Our Founding Fathers understood this, and they did not like it. They deliberately strove to create a different kind of system that would protect the people from the worst abuses of government. They knew that some government was necessary, but they sought to put it in a very small cage and on a very short leash. By enhancing the power of the individual, they spread the power across a very large base and prohibited it from being concentrated where the worst of the worst of us could acquire and wield it to everyone else's disadvantage. By giving vent to the selfish tendencies of all, they effectively neutralized the chances of oppression by the few. Would there still be problems? Of course. Would there still be imperfections? Obviously. Would there still be suffering and injustice? Inevitably. But in all cases the harmful effects which would result from a system of decentralized power would be far less than the harmful effects which would derive from a system of centralized power.

Sadly, we have forgotten the wisdom of the Founders. We listened to the siren's song of the foolish and the wicked. They pointed to the problems, the imperfections, the suffering, and the injustices. They promised that we could do better. All we had to do is concentrate more power so it could be used to overcome these social evils. They praised the wonders that could be accomplished by a benevolent, big government. In theory they were right; but in practice, a big government never stays benevolent for very long. Never. Great power gives great vent to the holders of that power; and given the selfish, corrupt nature of man, that's just not going to work out too well for most of us. What's more, a new dynamic will begin to work. Not only will great power give great vent to the great selfishness of those who hold that power, great power itself will attract the worst of the worst of us – the most selfish of the selfish – like a steaming pile of manure attracts all manner of vile insects. Creating a big government baits the hook and attracts the most abominably wicked of our kind. Unfortunately, they aren't the ones who end up getting caught, skinned, and gutted. We are.

In summary, one of the best ways to live free and to prevent becoming the victim of another's selfish nature is to minimize the accumulation of power – everywhere – but especially in the realms of government, economics, and religion.

(2) The first way to minimize the harm done by our selfish natures is to minimize the power available to those who have such a nature – which is pretty much all of us. The second way to minimize the harm is to change our nature. This is the more comprehensive and permanent

of the two options. It also is the more difficult. Still, it is not only worth pursuing, it is absolutely essential. You see, an immoral people cannot long remain a free people. It simply cannot happen. Our Founders understood this. This is why they were so concerned with the moral and spiritual development of the people. They saw a necessary interaction that was imperative to preserve "the land of the free." A good government can only derive from a good people; and a good people must be encouraged and nurtured by a good government.

Embedded in the preceding paragraph is a critical premise that *must* be remembered and factored into any plans for social engineering: *an immoral people cannot long remain a free people*. The declaration here is this: a free society can only be enjoyed and preserved by a moral populace. The implication that derives from this declaration is that a populace must work to preserve morality if it hopes to preserve its liberties.

There is no question that the Founders generally believed this. John Adams summed up their conviction quite nicely when he wrote, "Statesmen, my dear Sir, may plan and speculate for liberty, but it is religion and morality alone which can establish the principles upon which freedom can securely stand. The only foundation of a free constitution is pure virtue." The Founders' wisdom flowed into the next generation when Robert Winthrop, Speaker of the House of Representatives for the thirtieth Congress in the 1840s, summed it up like this: "Men, in a word, must necessarily be controlled either by a power within them or by a power without them; either by the Word of God or by the strong arm of man; either by the Bible or by the bayonet."

Yes, there is no question that the Founders believed that an immoral people cannot long remain a free people; but were they right? The vanguard of hedonistic America would argue a different case. They proclaim, "If it feels good, do it!" After all, what's the point of having freedom if you cannot use it? The Founders, on the other hand, would counter that if you don't use your freedom responsibly, you won't have it for very long.

So, were the Founders just a bunch of puritanic kill-joys who wanted to impose a hapless lifestyle on others, or were they sagacious sages who pointed the way to an enduring joy? I believe the answer to two simple questions will settle the matter quite conclusively. First, what do you think would happen if we gave a great deal of personal liberty to an immoral people? The answer is obvious. They will do immoral things, and the population will devolve into a penitentiary society – a nation occupied by criminals, but without the benefit of the bars and guards to restrain them. I think that all but the most perverse of us would agree that this would not be a good place in which to live. Second, what do you think would happen if we set up a limited, relatively weak government to rule over such an immoral populace? Again, the answer is obvious. You will have chaos, havoc, anarchy – and eventually despotism because the people will not long tolerate the profound instability which would characterize such a society. They will quickly sell out to the first strongman who promises safety. That, too, is a recurrent theme of history.

Let us conclude our brief study of the inevitable consequences of immorality by using Winthrop's model. If moral conviction (the Bible) does not drive a peoples' behavior, then they will be driven by their selfish interests. This puts everyone at odds with everyone else, which leads to riot and chaos. This, however, is an intolerable situation, and the people will soon turn to a despot who can reestablish a measure of order and safety. Of course, he will have to do this forcefully and violently (the bayonet). Personal freedom will become a scarcely remembered relic of the past.

An immoral people cannot long remain a free people. There is nothing especially profound about this revelation. One does not have to be a great philosopher to appreciate it. Almost every parent understands the principle here. You simply cannot entrust young children with a great deal of freedom. They are not ready to use it responsibly. Only morally responsible people – of any age – can be entrusted with freedom. Therefore, if you love liberty, you must preach and achieve morality.

Morality – true morality – is indispensable to the survival and success of a great and free nation. Now the question is, "What is morality?"

The first thing we need to know about true morality is that it is not man-made. Humans give us philosophy. Only God can create morality. Humans give us opinions.

God gives us truth. The works of humans are fickle and fleeting. The works of God are unchanging and eternal.

Now, it has been said that what God giveth God can taketh away, but He never changes what is right and what is wrong. That is not the case with men. What man giveth man can and probably will taketh away – even concepts of right and wrong. You see, the problem with secular, humanist, man-made concepts of morality is that they are conditional and relativistic – which means you cannot count on them. They change – often unpredictably. They can be one thing yesterday, a different thing today, and yet something else tomorrow. It can be one thing for you and another for me. How can you build on such an unstable foundation? You cannot. But that is not the case with true morality. True morality is the same yesterday, today, and tomorrow; and true morality is the same for one and all. True morality does not change. It is universal. It is eternal. It is from God and God alone. And if a nation is to be blessed by true morality, then that nation must be founded upon, rooted in, and springing up from "the laws of nature and of nature's God….", which is precisely what is proclaimed in our founding document, the Declaration of Independence.

The Founders were quite clear about their understanding of the source of true morality: it was from what they frequently called "true religion", which they unashamedly and unequivocally pronounced to be Christianity. The following statement by Noah Webster expresses the conviction held by many of our Founders. "[T]he Christian religion, in its purity, is the basis, or rather the source of all genuine freedom in government… and I am persuaded that no civil government of a republican form can exist and be durable in which the principles of that religion have not a controlling influence."

So, let us summarize this cascading flow of historic inevitability. Man's nature is essentially selfish. He is willing to exploit and abuse others for personal gain. The only thing necessary for this inclination to become realized is power. Man is still selfish and corrupt without power, but with power he can act on his intentions. Accordingly, it is profoundly dangerous and colossally foolish to allow the accumulation and concentration of great power. Wise social engineers work diligently to prevent this amassing of might. Fools and the wicked work diligently to accomplish it. Usually, the fools and the wicked prevail. This is why the historian is witness to a nearly universal phenomenon, which is our "First Law of Political History": Throughout the centuries, across the continents, within all cultures, the state will become the tool of a small minority who seek to oppress and plunder the productive majority. The surest way to prevent this abuse is to change the nature of man, and the best guide for accomplishing this is Christianity. This, however, is a tall order and will never be accomplished absolutely. Accordingly, it would be wise to have a backup plan in the event the remolding of human nature proves to be a protracted affair or fails altogether. This "Plan B" must inevitably work toward the decentralization of power – not its accumulation and concentration. In modern America, however, neither objective is being pursued. In fact, both are being aggressively opposed. The values and beliefs of Christianity are being assailed and undermined while we turn over more and more areas of our lives to the government, thereby encouraging its growth. This is an infallible plan for the inevitable collapse of a free America. Now, think about who would be interested in accomplishing this? Have you been voting for them?

The concentration of power and the abrogation of personal liberties were antithetical to the beliefs of our honorable and wise Founders. On the other hand, the concentration of power and the abrogation of personal liberties is an irresistible attraction to the less scrupulous and more foolish. These have also been the goals of our avowed enemies. The Socialistic concentration of power that has characterized America's political evolution in recent decades serves the interests of the unscrupulous very well. In fact, the treacherous politician is about the only one whose interests are served by Socialism. Socialism has an unequalled record of failure, but it does a masterful job of gathering power in one convenient location where the unprincipled abusers of humankind can seize it and use it to serve their interests.

Given our First and Second Laws of Political History, we must conclude that those who grapple against the growth of big government are among our greatest heroes; and those who promote the growth of big government are among our greatest villains.

Look around. The villains are winning.

The Third Law of Political History. *The same factors which propel a nation to greatness will also plant the seeds for its eventual collapse.*

The rise of great Powers can result from a variety of circumstances; but once the rise has taken place, a very singular course is nearly inevitable – and fatal. Power leads to wealth which leads to comfort which leads to sloth which leads to decline, defeat, and dissolution. This phenomenon is easy to track in the record of history, but it is not easy for a comfortable people to combat. It simply takes too much effort and requires too much discipline and diligence. And since the catastrophic collapse does not seem imminent until it is too late to avoid, addressing it can always be postponed – and it usually is.

In this regard, national evolution mimics a pattern experienced by many successful individuals. As young adults, they work hard and keep their goals ever before them. They stay lean and mean. They live for tomorrow. Today, they struggle, scrimp, and save. Eventually, all the labor, sacrifice, and commitment pay off. They achieve the good life. But then they start to live the good life, and life goes bad. They become less physical, and the body grows soft. They eat unwisely, and the arteries grow hard. The paunch becomes noticeable, and the decision is made to address it – soon. Eventually, embarrassment, disgust, and the nagging of doctors and spouse inspire the desire to perspire and reclaim lost glories. A gym membership is purchased – along with a new wardrobe in spandex – and the latest diet craze is embraced. But results are hard to achieve and slow in coming. Meanwhile the enticements of debauchery are everywhere and compelling. The once victorious warrior surrenders – although he convinces himself that it is merely a tactical retreat. He assures himself that he will rise again but then falls back into his old habits. There may be a few more attempts at reform, but more likely the soon-to-be-victim convinces himself that he is immortal – until a vessel explodes in his brain, or a malignancy wastes him away to skeletal proportions, or he seizes his chest and drops to the floor with spittle flowing from the corner of his mouth.

The fruits of success for which we worked so hard will ultimately turn against us – *unless* we are ever vigilant and ever faithful to those core values which first honored us with glory. We must forever remember what we fought for and resist the tendency to become what we fought against. The lessons of success must be retaught, relearned, and repeated – endlessly. They are easy to write, easy to read, and easy to believe, but not easy to achieve – which is why every great civilization of the past is in the past.

*   *   *

Three laws, etched with iron into stone and woven into the very fabric of life. They are immutable and inescapable. So, are we doomed? That's up to us. Avoiding collapse will not be easy. It will require us to swim upstream, but the alternative is to float with the current and go over the falls. There is a way out, but it will not be found by doing more of the same. So, what is the answer?

If you are expecting an endorsement of the Republican Party, the Democratic Party, or any other political party, you will be disappointed. If you are looking for a call to embrace the philosophy of the left or of the right, you will be surprised. If you think you will be urged to adopt the tenets of conservatism or liberalism, think again. If you expect to hear a rehash of tired old ideas, you are wrong.

In the pages to follow, I believe that you will read things that you have never read nor heard before. They truly are revolutionary. This is very appropriate. In fact, it is necessary. America was born in revolution, and it will be re-born in revolution. The ineffectual philosophies, parties, programs, and personalities of today have proven themselves irrelevant to our needs. These, after all, are what (and who) have caused our problems. They have nothing to offer us but more of the same woe and grief that they have engendered. It is high time that they be deposited on the ash heap of history.

Our problems are great, but we are greater. America is not done. The stench which inflames our senses comes from the manure which our traitorous politicians have heaped upon this sacred land. But manure makes for fertile soil, and the politicians have unwittingly prepared the ground for the very new growth that will bury them.

Now, before we proceed to see how we will accomplish this, let us first pause briefly to assess the current political environment.

CHAPTER THREE

2012. ASHES.

On the morning of Wednesday, November 7, 2012, the American people awakened to walk amidst the wreckage of their once-great nation – and they didn't even know it. The incomprehensible had happened.

One political party proudly offered to the people a candidate who had amassed one of the worst records in our history – maybe *the* worst. By virtually all objective standards the administration of the previous four years had failed and failed miserably. It had even failed by standards it had set for itself.

The economy was in shambles. Despite trillions of dollars of "stimulation" through bailouts, payoffs, and "free" gifts, the economy was stagnant and unemployment was significantly higher than when the administration had initiated its "recovery" plan nearly four years earlier. Average household income was markedly lower than four years before. The national debt had soared at an unprecedented rate. The cost of staples, like fuel, had skyrocketed. A healthcare plan had been enacted that would cripple businesses and undermine the wellbeing of millions of Americans. Our entire economy was being made increasingly vulnerable to the malevolent schemes of foreign powers that were our confessed enemies. And while the indicators of economic peril pointed clearly to the need for meaningful reform, the administration continued to throw sand in the machinery of our economic engines – the free enterprise system. Instead of renovation, the administration continued to invest in a system of governmental control that has an unfailing record of failure.

In the arena of foreign relations, Uncle Sam had donned a clown suit and traipsed around the globe in big, clumsy shoes. We provided weapons to drug cartels working at and within our borders. We snubbed our friends and bowed to our adversaries. Uncle Vladimir was promised that we would be more "flexible" in the future when it came to protecting our people and our national interests. And while the President winked at the reincarnation of Soviet Stalinism, we exposed ourselves to mortal danger by allowing hostile lunatics, who are avowed enemies, to develop weapons of mass destruction and delivery devices which could reach our heartland. It never occurred to this somnolent administration that September 11 might be a good time to expect Islamic terrorists to strike again; and so in the very midst of the land of Islamic lunatics, we left our embassies, consulates, and related diplomatic offices nearly defenseless and vulnerable to attack. And when the inevitable happened – when American facilities were desecrated and decimated, Americans were killed, and the nation was shamed – the President provided his embattled countrymen with precious little assistance, blamed the whole thing on a third-rate video, and then went off to campaign for the privilege to impose four more years of incompetence upon our people.

But worse than all of this, the morals of America – the bedrock of any nation's wellbeing, prosperity, and security – were not only allowed to decay, they were encouraged to do so. At the dedication – the consecration – of our nation, President George Washington warned that "the propitious smiles of Heaven can never be expected on a nation that disregards the eternal rules of order and right which Heaven itself has ordained...." He was right, and he was not alone. Virtually all of the Founding Fathers were devout, practicing Christians who understood the connection between morality and the pursuit and achievement of personal and national happiness. These were learned and wise men who had gleaned the wisdom of the ages. One of their philosophical mentors had been Sir William Blackstone who wrote,

"Man, considered as a creature, must necessarily be subject to the laws of his Creator, for he is entirely a dependent being.... And, consequently, as man depends absolutely upon his Maker for everything, it is necessary that he should in all points conform to his

Maker's will ... this will of his Maker is called the law of nature.

"These laws laid down by God are the eternal immutable laws of good and evil....This law of nature dictated by God himself, is of course superior in obligation to any other. It is binding over all the globe, in all countries, and at all times: no human laws are of any validity if contrary to this....

"The doctrines thus delivered we call the revealed or divine law, and they are to be found only in the holy scriptures... [and] are found upon comparison to be really part of the original law of nature. Upon these two foundations, the law of nature and the law of revelation, depend all human laws: that is to say, no human laws should be suffered to contradict these." (Taken from Blackstone's *Commentaries on the Laws of England*.)

Holy Scripture is the fount of true morality, and true morality is the foundation of a well-ordered and prosperous nation. Despite this truth and the wisdom of the Founders who appreciated it, recent national leaders and the administration of 2008 and 2012 have opted for a different course – the path of fools, the way of wickedness. The President wasted little time – in fact he seemed to relish the opportunity to declare that the United States was not a Christian nation. By doing so, he betrayed our heritage and spat in the face of God. He then linked arms and marched boldly forward with the dolts and demons who witlessly or wittingly work for our nation's decline and fall. God has been expelled from our schools and exiled from other areas of public life. Prayer is prohibited while profanity and pornography are promoted. The Ten Commandments are crated up and carted off. Innocent lives are slaughtered by the millions because they are inconvenient. Marriage is redefined and undermined instead of reinforced and undisputed. "One nation under God" and "In God We Trust" have become inconvenient slogans of a bygone age instead of guiding principles for today and tomorrow.

It was a record of nearly total failure. Even the party in power couldn't spin things vigorously enough to run on its own accomplishments. There were virtually none. The Democrats could do no better than to offer a rerun of what was arguably the most disastrous presidential administration in our history. The Republicans couldn't even offer that much – at least in the eyes of the people. It should have been easy pickings for the Republicans. The presidency, up for grabs in the election of November, 2012, presented itself as low-hanging fruit that even a bumbling incompetent should have been able to snatch. The result?

America lost.

Is this to say that Americans made the wrong choice in selecting who would serve as President for the next four years? No. Rather, it is to say that there really was no choice.

Across the political spectrum there is one thing on which most Americans agree: the nation is a mess. The dispute is mostly about who is responsible for the mess and what should be done about it.

Let us consider the first question: who is responsible for the mess? Is it the Democrats? Is it the Republicans? The answer is, "Yes."

The Republicans and Democrats constitute the political tag-team that has presided over the unfolding calamity of our beloved America. They are the ones who have been in charge for the last century-and-a-half, so who else could be responsible?

Next question: what should be done about correcting their mess? Should we turn to the problem-causers to be the problem-solvers? That just doesn't sound very hopeful to any reasonable observer. If "they" knew how to solve the problems, then why did "they" create them in the first place?

Many of us grew up in families where one of the house rules was, "If you make a mess, clean it up." Now, perhaps if the Democrats and Republicans actually offered us genuinely new solutions, we might consider giving them another chance; but they don't. *Listen* to what they say. It hasn't changed for generations. They don't offer Americans any true choice. They merely offer unscrupulous politicians different vehicles for advancing their careers at our expense; and frankly, their proposals aren't much different from each other. The only true choice they offer is the speed at which we race toward oblivion.

We elect Republicans and things get worse. We switch to the Democrats and things get worse. We get fed up and go back to the Republicans, and things get worse. It must be time for a change; so we try the Democrats, and things get worse. Furthermore, the political system itself has become almost entirely dysfunctional. Members of the two dominant parties spend most of their time and expend most of their energy butting heads instead of extending hands – not that it would make much difference to us if they were more compromising. The fact is, they both are wrong; and when wrong compromises with wrong, guess what you get. That's right: wrong.

The current political system is a fiasco, and the Democrats and Republicans are both bankrupt. They have not only failed us, they have betrayed us. Up until a couple of decades ago, we could be gracious and conclude that, at best, they were good-hearted but wrong-headed. Perhaps they had bought into nice sounding notions for social justice and national prosperity, but erred – grievously – and we the people had been hoodwinked into trusting them. However, there are no longer any grounds to be gracious. The error of their ways has been abundantly obvious for some time now, and the only reason for them to continue to pursue these pathways is because they are completely incapable of conceiving any new ideas, or because they have found ways to profit from the old ones – which means that they benefit from our suffering. In short, they are either incompetent or evil. We no longer can afford to entrust them with our lives, our fortunes, and our futures; and since there is no other viable option, we'll just have to create one of our own.

We the people have had it! Republicans, Democrats, you're fired! We don't trust you any more, and we are taking back control of our lives, our fortunes, and our destiny. The only change we can believe in is to change the way we look at government, to change the way that government runs, and to change the people who will run it. Your old ways have brought us to the point of ruin. It is time to leave the "left" and to admit the "right" is wrong. We must begin anew.

The main purposes of this book are

1. to acknowledge the hopelessness of trusting the establishment political parties
2. to replace the Left-Right paradigm with a new model for guiding political action
3. to reveal the philosophy of government that inspired our Founders
4. to use this philosophy to resurrect, preserve, protect, and defend the Constitution
5. to develop new initiatives for reforming our land
6. to found new organizations for accomplishing our objectives
7. to restore genuine hope for meaningful reform
8. to consider an alternative history of the future from the one being prepared for us
9. to rebuild America the Great and to secure its future for our children and theirs

Our mission is to reclaim our nation; to rebuild the United States according to our founding principles; to restore its greatness and glory.

We will create a new way, we will begin a new movement, and we will forge a new America.

We will arise!

CHAPTER FOUR

THE EMPTY QUIVER

For those unfamiliar with archery, the "quiver" is an elongated pouch used to hold arrows. It is usually slung across the upper back of the archer so his ordnance is within easy reach. To the warriors of old, however, it was more than just a bag. A full quiver was a symbol and meter of survivability and hope. A quiver full of arrows gave the archer a chance of success and survival. He could fight for his cause, fight against his enemy, and maybe save his life. A full quiver offered hope that he could accomplish his mission and survive. On the other hand, an empty quiver was the harbinger of doom. If the warrior had expended all his bolts, it surely meant that the battle was still raging, but he had nothing left with which to fight the enemy and defend himself. The empty quiver was the symbol of defeat, hopelessness, and imminent death.

It still is.

The empty quiver has come to symbolize the prospects of modern America – at least, as long as we continue to invest our hopes for the future with the two "establish-ment" political parties. Remember, these are the parties that have been in control for the last century-and-a-half. These are the parties which are responsible for the cur-rent crisis – there is no one else to blame. And these are the parties which offer us nothing different from the bad medicine which they have prescribed for decades. It was this medicine which made us sick in the first place. Is there any reason to hope that more of the same will have different results in the future?

Now, to be sure, the leaders of those two parties will tell a different tale. They will have us believe that they have come up with something new and hopeful – a change that we can believe in. The sad reality is that they spend far more time in marketing than in imagin-ing. They are experts in repackaging, not reform. They simply take the same, old pile that they have been shov-eling for years and put it in a different box, give it a new ribbon and bow, and slap a sticker on it that says, "New and Improved!" In reality, the only thing new about it is the sticker.

We the people cannot help but wonder why this is. Are they so bereft of creative thinking that they are in-capable of coming up with new ideas for addressing our crisis; or have they found a way to profit from our misery and actually want to perpetuate it? Could it be that they have decided that all they need to do is stay the course and merely look as though they are concerned and work-ing to solve our problems? Well, that sounds rather harsh;

and it smacks of the kind of thing a nutty, conspiratorial theorist would conceive. Still, have you noticed that no matter which way the election goes, they win and we lose? They get the power, the prestige, and the privileges, while we suffer debt, disappointment, and disillusionment. They get luxury healthcare and pensions, while we lose our own and get to pay for theirs. They destroy jobs and the economy, and then grant themselves the power to reach deeper into our pockets to pay for their mistakes. They heap mounds of rules and regulations on us while exempting themselves from having to obey these same requirements. Yes, no matter which way the election goes, they win, we lose. Maybe that nutty, conspiratorial theorist isn't so crazy after all.

The Democratic and Republican Parties have nothing to offer us but more of the same formula for disaster that they have used to bring this great land and its people to the brink of collapse. If they were honest, they would trade in the jack ass and the elephant for the empty quiver; but, they are not honest, and we would be fools of the highest order to continue to follow them.

Imagine a man who goes to his doctor because he is deathly ill. The doctor conducts a series of tests and determines that the man is suffering from a bad case of arsenic poisoning. He tells his patient this, then hands him a prescription. "Here, this should take care of you."

"Oh, thank you, doctor", the patient exclaims. He continues, "What's this for?", looking at the prescription.

The doctor smiles and says, "Arsenic."

"Arsenic!" The patient is incredulous. "Didn't you say that arsenic is what was making me sick?"

The doctor, still smiling, says, "Yes."

"And you want me to take more?"

"Yes."

"And you honestly think this is going to make me better?"

"Trust me. I'm a doctor." He holds out his hand and says, "That'll be fifty bucks."

Any prudent patient would fire that physician on the spot, and that would be good advice for us. The Republicans and the Democrats have rendered themselves irrelevant to our futures. It is high time we fire them and their failed ideas and move on to something that actually works. But what? Well, how about something that actually worked?

Before we proceed with putting some new arrows in our empty quiver, let us pause a moment to clear the decks for action. We need to sweep away some musty, old conceptions which not only have crept their way into our thinking – they have come to dominate the way we perceive politics and political solutions.

CHAPTER FIVE

THE PERILOUS PARADIGM

Stop for a moment and think about your political beliefs. Now think about where you would position yourself on the "Left-Right" scale of political thinking. Are you far left of center, a little left of center, a centrist, a little right of center, or far right of center?

Far Left   Leftish   Center   Rightish   Far Right

Your answer to that question may be a big part of our problem.

The "solvability" of a problem often has more to do with how one perceives the problem than with the difficulty of the problem. For example, my wife suffered from allergies for many years. Her "western" doctors with their "western" ways told her that her only options were to avoid the allergens or to drug her symptoms into a stupor with medications that often caused more ailments than they alleviated. Then she discovered an "eastern" physician with an "eastern" perspective, and her allergies were cured. Yes, cured; and without the use of harmful drugs or painful needles. The solution to her problem wasn't especially difficult. In fact, being cured from an allergy took scarcely one day and required no exotic nor expensive treatments. The solution was easy. The hard part was finding the correct perception of the problem – the perspective that would lead to a solution. As long as she relied on doctors with a western perspective, our only hope was to invest in the stocks of the pharmaceutical companies that were making a fortune off the sale of ineffective drugs.

The tale of Christopher Columbus is another, better-known example. Fifteenth century Europeans craved the riches of the Orient, which was to the east. So, how do you get to the east? Head east, of course. There were a few pesky problems, though; like the need to deal with thousands of miles of mountains and valleys and deserts and rivers and unfriendly government officials and robbers (but then, I repeat myself). There was an alternative. One could sail to the east, but there was a little obstacle called "Africa" that got in the way – not to mention pirates. But Columbus thought "outside the box." He reasoned that if the world were a big ball, then one could reach the east by sailing west. His solution was brilliantly simple, and it would have worked except for another little obstacle called the "Americas."

The point is this: the inaccurate perception of a problem will almost always complicate and frustrate the solution of a problem. An accurate perception of a problem will facilitate a solution. I believe that one of the reasons why we have found many socio-political problems so intractable is because we have an inaccurate perception of the political situation. We perceive politics in terms of "Left" or "Right", and accordingly we think of solutions in terms of moving to the left or moving to the right. But what if this model, or "paradigm", were fundamentally flawed? If it is, then we will find no true solutions as long as we remain wedded to the "Left-Right Paradigm." I believe the paradigm *is* flawed and that the time has come to leave the left and admit the right is wrong.

The terms "left" and "right" were first used to describe political ideologies during the time of the French Revolution. In 1789 the old "Estates-General" evolved into the new "National Assembly" and essentially served as the French parliament. The representatives of the nobility tended to sit on one side of the hall while the commoners sat on the other. From the perspective of the presiding officer, who faced the representatives, the nobles were to the right and the commoners to the left. Consequently, when the presiding officer gave permission for someone to speak, he often referred to the "gentleman on the left" (if a commoner) or the "gentleman on the right" (if a noble).

Originally, the term "leftist" tended to be associated with those who supported greater liberty and power for the commoners, while the term "rightists" was associated with those who wished to preserve the power of the nobles. In time, however, this began to change. Starting around the period of the European revolutions of 1848, "leftism" came to be associated increasingly with Marxist and related socialist ideologies. These philosophies consistently promoted the establishment of powerful governmental institutions in order to accomplish reforms. "Rightism", on the other hand, came to be associated with those who sought to promote the exercise of individual liberties by protecting them from the abuses of big government. This new ideological orientation would twist the definitions of the "left-right paradigm" to a point where the terms have now shifted almost 180 degrees from their original meaning. Currently, the leftists are inclined to rely on a governmental approach to solving social problems. They seek to grow the government and expand its power over many areas of the people's lives. The rightists see government as one of the greatest dangers to the exercise of individual liberties. They seek to shrink the government and expand the people's power to control the affairs of their own lives. Leftists think the people will be better off if a big, powerful, and benevolent government protects the people and manages their affairs. Rightists think the people will be better off if they are allowed to fend for themselves and manage their own affairs.

As a consequence, the modern "Left-Right Paradigm" is perceived largely in terms of how much government a people should have. The extreme left position is represented by total government, or "totalitarianism." The extreme right position is represented by no government, or "anarchy."

<u>Totalitarianism</u>   <u>Center</u>   <u>Anarchy</u>

Most people agree that the extremes are undesirable. Under "totalitarianism" there is no individual freedom and everyone fears his government. Under "anarchy" there is unrestrained freedom and everyone fears his neighbor. Both extremes are socially toxic. We might think of totalitarianism as arsenic and anarchy as cyanide. The consensus opinion is that the "best" position is somewhere on the line between the two extremes; but is any mixture of arsenic and cyanide healthy?

The current understanding of the "Left-Right Paradigm" offers us no true solutions because it relates almost exclusively to method instead of mission. The argument has focused on how much government we need instead of the goals of that government. As long as we stick with the current paradigm, we will be stuck with the current load of problems. Just as my wife needed someone with a different perspective to cure her allergies, America – and the world at large – needs a different perspective to cure its diseases. Instead of "Right-Left", I recommend "Up-Down."

In the Up-Down Paradigm the emphasis is not on the size of government but rather on accomplishing certain principle-based goals. This is not to say that the size of government is irrelevant. It is tremendously relevant. (Remember the *First* and *Second Laws of Political History*.)

The fact is, however, that one size does not fit all. There is not one ideal size of government that is most appropriate under all circumstances. Times of dire crisis, like a major war, may justify an increase in the size and power of government. Times of peace and prosperity will require the government to recede, or it will interfere with both peace and prosperity. Still, what we will find is that the size issue will tend to naturally resolve itself if the proper principles are honored and accomplished. So now the question is, "What are the proper principles? What does it mean to head 'Upward'?"

CHAPTER SIX

ARISE!

In the last chapter we discussed the problems with the "Left-Right Paradigm." As it currently stands, this universally accepted model relates primarily to method rather than mission. It argues the question of how much government is desirable rather than the question of what the government should be doing. Size does matter, but purpose matters even more; and when the question of purpose is rightly answered, the answer to the question of size will follow naturally. Of course, there is another problem with the "Left-Right Paradigm." If one is forever focused on shifting to the right or to the left, one will never ascend. The time has come for America to arise.

The political philosophy of "Ascendancy" is mission-oriented. At its heart is this question: What is the proper purpose of government?" So, let's get to it. What is the rightful role of the state?

The answer of America – and, I believe, the ultimate answer for all peoples – was stated succinctly in 1776 and is found in the second paragraph of the Declaration of Independence. It was important to the colonists to justify their decision to separate themselves from Great Britain "and to assume among the Powers of the earth, the separate and equal station" of an independent nation. They wanted the world and history to understand that this decision was not taken lightly nor was it taken for reasons of greed or expediency. Their action was rooted in and justified by nothing less than "the Laws of Nature and of Nature's God...." Their act of rebellion was legitimate because the behavior of the British government had become illegitimate. Parliament and the King had violated "the Laws of Nature and of Nature's God," and accordingly, the covenant between the mother country and her colonies was broken – by Britain, not us. But, what were "the Laws of Nature and of Nature's God" as they pertained to government? This was critical. How could we claim that Great Britain had broken its covenant with us unless we clearly described what that covenant was? If we were going to charge another with illegitimate behavior, we first had to define what is "legitimacy." Accordingly, we *had* to proclaim a philosophy of government in the Declaration, and so we did. Unfortunately, most modern-day Americans are oblivious to it. Ironically, it is hidden in plain sight. In fact, the heart and soul of this philosophy are presented in the most memorized lines in the document. Thomas Jefferson, the main author of the Declaration, wasted no time in addressing this issue.

We hold these truths to be self-evident, that all men are created equal, that they are endowed by their Creator with certain unalienable Rights, that among these are Life, Liberty and the pursuit of Happiness. That to secure these rights, Governments are instituted among Men, deriving their just powers from the consent of the governed, That whenever any Form of Government becomes destructive of these ends, it is the Right of the People to alter or to abolish it, and to institute new Government, laying its foundation on such principles and organizing its powers in such form, as to them shall seem most likely to effect their Safety and Happiness.

Let us now consider this brilliantly concise statement point by point. We must ensure that this philosophy of legitimate government is properly understood so that it may be properly applied. This is, after all, how we were intended to organize and operate our government.

We hold these truths to be self-evident....

The wise and learned men who drafted and approved the Declaration knew that this proclamation was based on truths that were self-evident. Perhaps they were assuming a bit much; but one must lay a sound foundation for any act of construction, and there generally will be certain necessary assumptions built into any foundation. The Founders assumed that the statements which were to follow would or should be obvious and acceptable. To put it bluntly, if you don't see the veracity of these claims, you are probably either too poorly educated or too downright stupid to be considering these matters at all. You would be well-advised to leave it to those who have minds better than yours. Of course, if you are that stupid, you probably won't appreciate the wisdom of that advice. (I told you this would be blunt.)

...all men are created equal, that they are endowed by their Creator with certain unalienable Rights....

The rights of mankind are granted by no one less than God Himself – "their Creator." They are unalienable, which means that since God granted them, only God can rightfully revoke them. Governments may not annul nor limit these rights without assailing the work of God and challenging His ultimate authority. When any government affronts the work of God and abridges the rights of humankind, it renders itself illegitimate and may be altered or abolished by the people – peacefully or otherwise as the need arises.

All men are created equally, at least in terms of their entitlement to exercise certain unalienable rights. People may not look the same; they may have differing natures and capabilities; they may be born into or acquire different stations in life, but they all are entitled to the equal exercise of their God-given rights. To be sure, this is not a guarantee of equal outcome, but it is a guarantee of the legal opportunity to exercise these rights the same as everyone else. There is absolutely no intent here to pursue nor commit to the equal distribution of the wealth of the nation. The Founders were not attempting to create a cookie-cutter society where everyone got the same amount and type of cookies. They did want to create a society where everyone was free to bake and/or buy as many cookies as he could earn.

There is another important element to this grant of equal rights that must not be overlooked. To say that "all men are created equal" means, among other things, that from the moment a person is created, that person is entitled to the same protection of his rights as any other person. That protection continues throughout the remainder of his life. This means that a just-conceived fetus is as entitled to the exercise of his God-given rights as a one-year old, a twenty-one year old, or a hundred-and-one year old – and the most solemn and sacred job of the government is to defend these rights. It is clear, therefore, that there is no right to abortion. More on this later and in the chapter on "Linkage."

... that among these are Life, Liberty and the pursuit of Happiness.

Something strange happened here. Jefferson and the others who approved the Declaration here omitted one of the Holy Trinity of Fundamental Rights usually accepted by the Founders (and by Jefferson himself in his other writings): the right of property. The usual claim was that the basic rights were life, property, and liberty. The reasoning went like this: Above all, one must have life. Without life all other considerations are moot – even pointless. Rocks don't need governments. Next, one must have property. In its most elemental form, "property" will even include one's own body and the labor performed by that body. Beyond this, property includes such essentials as food, drink, clothing, and shelter. Property also consists of items like tools, land, buildings, and a variety of other supplies necessary to sustain the first right, which is life. Now that one has life and property, one needs the liberty necessary to use his life and property in order to pursue his happiness. Without liberty, the individual will never arise above the status of a slave. His life and property will never be his own, and the pursuit of happiness will be impossible.

Technically speaking, the "pursuit of happiness" is not a right. It is a consequence of practicing the other three fundamental rights. Establishing the "pursuit of happiness" as an unalienable right would open Pandora's Box and unleash all manner of evil into society. Virtually any behavior – like molesting children, abusing the elderly, torture, rape, murder, theft, etc. – could be logically justified by the perpetrator if he simply argued that these activities made him happy. Such a "right" to pursue one's happiness would devour the other rights and unhinge the society.

It is vitally important to keep the following distinctions in mind: One is not promised life, but rather the *right to* life. One is not promised property, but rather the *right to* property. One is not promised liberty, but rather the *right to* liberty. What's the difference? The Founders did not intend to guarantee an outcome – only the opportunity to pursue an outcome. Rather than attempting to mandate a specific result (like a chicken in every pot, a car in every garage, jobs for all, healthcare for all, or pensions for all), the Founders wisely sought instead to promote procedural fairness which allows individuals to rise to the level of their gifts and guts. Promising results is a game played by fools and the crooks who prey upon them.

One has the *right to* life, but not the guarantee that life will be preserved. One might use his liberty foolishly or abusively and lose his life – or even lose the right to life if one uses his liberty to endanger, abuse, or destroy another's rights. One has the *right to* property, but not the guarantee that property will be acquired or preserved once it is acquired. One might use his liberty foolishly or abusively and lose his property – or even lose the right to property if one uses his liberty to endanger, abuse, or destroy another's rights. One has the *right to* liberty, but not the guarantee that he will always enjoy the exercise of liberty. One might lose his liberty if he uses it to endanger, abuse, or destroy another's rights. Again, there is no guarantee of outcome, only the guarantee of opportunity.

Furthermore, there is no guarantee that all will enjoy equal opportunity. The only mention of equality here is in the possession of rights. We "are created equal" in that we all receive a guarantee to the same basic rights, but we do not all receive an equal opportunity to use those rights. For example, we all are entitled to the right of life, but some will be born with superior physical and mental attributes that will allow them to more easily attain the blessings of life than is the case with others who are disadvantaged. It is not the role of government to compensate for the differential opportunity endowed by the Creator at birth or thereafter. We all are entitled to the right of property, but this does not mean that we all shall either start out with or end up with the same amount and type of property. It simply means that we are entitled to acquire, keep, use, and transfer personal property; and that no one is entitled to abridge nor alienate that right unless we use our right in a manner that works to abridge or alienate the rights of another. We all are entitled to the right of liberty, but some will be born with or will acquire the opportunity to get more out of their exercise of liberty than others. Again, the only guarantee is that all will receive these rights, not the guarantee that all will have an equal opportunity to derive benefits from these rights. In effect, the Founders are saying that the door is open to all. Some will start off closer to the door than others; some will pass through the door and travel farther than others; some will pass through the door then turn around and go back; and some will never get to the door. The only concern of the government is to keep the door open.

That to secure these rights, Governments are instituted among Men....

These ten words are profoundly critical, and they must be read in conjunction with the preceding passages. Together they speak to the most basic assertion regarding the legitimate and proper purpose of government, and yet the significance of these words is generally over-looked. If we are searching for the rightful role of government, here it is; and in case you missed it, read these passages backwards.

"Governments are instituted among Men" "to secure these rights" "that ... are endowed by their Creator...." There it is in a nice, neat nutshell. Governments exist to do the work of God. (Kind of pulls the rug out from under that old "separation of church and state" nonsense, doesn't it?) And the specific work of God that governments must address above all others is the protection of "these rights" with which the Creator has endowed us. This is the foremost responsibility of government, and if a government fails to do this, or actively works against this, it is illegitimate and deserves to be altered or abolished.

It's all about rights and the protection of these rights. From the moment of conception, every human is entitled to certain rights – the sacred Trinity of which are Life, Property, and Liberty. We know that others exist, for the drafters agreed "that *among* these are Life, Liberty and the pursuit of Happiness." (Emphasis added.) But whatever the comprehensive list of rights may be (more on that later), we do know that a government's most vital purpose is to defend these. All the same, government is not the *first* defender of these rights. In fact, it normally should be the last line of defense.

The rights-holder will usually be the first responder when it comes to the defense of one's own rights. The role of the government is to back up the rights-holder when he is unable to successfully defend his rights himself. Before we give an example of how this often will work, it is important to discuss another vital aspect of the defense of rights.

There is a "sacred covenant" among all rights-holders that must be honored. This "sacred covenant" requires that one's rights may not be used to deny the rights of another. Now, it is true that the legitimate exercise of one's rights may impinge upon the successful exercise of another's rights, but one may not materially deny the rights of another. For example, suppose I operate a restaurant with better food and better service than another restaurant in town. Because of my superior operation, I am more successful than my competitor. He may even be forced to close, but this is not a violation of his rights. He had an opportunity just like I did. I did not deny him an opportunity – I just made more of my opportunity than he did, and he suffered a predictable consequence. No problem here. However, if I sabotaged my competitor's operation, fire-bombed his building, or used my friendship with the mayor to impose regulations on him that did not apply to me, then there is a problem. The "sacred covenant" must be honored by all rights-holders or the violator's rights may be revoked or abridged. Now, let us look at an example of how the defense of one's rights – and the government's role in this defense – may play out.

Suppose my neighbor decides that he likes my car better than his own. He doesn't want to settle for his old clunker any longer, but he also doesn't wish to go to the trouble and expense of buying another vehicle. Being bereft of morals, he tries to take my car – a violation of my property rights. I am entitled to defend my property. Since he has abused his right to liberty by using that liberty in an attempt to deny or abridge the rights of another, he has broken the "sacred covenant" and forfeited his rights. I am rightfully entitled to use my rights to defend my rights, even if it means that my neighbor's rights are violated. I am entitled to thwart him. I am morally (and conceivably legally) obligated to begin at the low end of the scale of resistance, like politely asking him to stop. If that fails, I am entitled to escalate my resistance until the neighbor has given up his illegitimate efforts to take my property or until I decide to seek assistance in my quest to defend my property. I may ask other family members, friends, or neighbors to assist me in keeping my property; but if this effort is unsuccessful, my last resort is government. The primary job of government at all levels is to defend the rights of individuals and groups when they are unable to do so for themselves.

... deriving their just powers from the consent of the governed...

First, a definition: power is the ability to do something – to achieve a result. Power may be used constructively or destructively. It may be used for good or evil. The goal has nothing to do with the existence of power. Power, simply, is the ability to get something done. If you can do something, you have power – if you can't, you don't. There are several types of power. In this particular passage of the Declaration, the concern of the Founders is with "just power."

Governments derive their "just powers" from the consent of those whom it governs. Another word for "just powers" is "authority." Not all power is authority. "Authority" is legitimate power, and frankly, most governments throughout history have not had legitimate power. "Authority" is not raw strength. It is power that has received legitimacy from some noble source. In the case of the Declaration, the noble source is the consent of the governed. In other words, there are governments that rule without the consent of the governed; but they do not have authority and are, therefore, either illegitimate or administrators of an immature society. (More on the issue of "maturity" later.)

As simple as this may seem, it is not. First of all, "consent" merely implies permission. The governed may not be thrilled about everything the government does, but if the people have granted permission to do something, then the government has the "consent" of the governed. But does this consent always result in "just power" or "authority?" This is where it gets dicey. According to the Founders, the answer was an emphatic "No!" Permission does not always grant legitimacy and create authority.

The second paragraph of the Declaration of Independence is a brilliantly concise statement regarding the proper role of government, but we cannot expect something this brief to flesh out all the necessary details of governing – and as they say, the devil is in the details.

Here we need to consider some other notions that were "self-evident" to the Founders but which may escape the attention of many mere modern-day mortals. Let us look at the issue of "consent" in light of the difference between "democracies" and "republics."

The Founders were acutely aware of the distinction between a "democracy" and a "republic." Despite common misperceptions, the Founders had no desire to create a democracy. Democracies always fail; they fail because of a fatal flaw; and the death is usually ugly. The Founders didn't want this for their new creation. They wanted a republic. What's the difference?

There is a well-known quote that is often attributed to Benjamin Franklin. It states that "Democracy is two wolves and a lamb voting on what to have for lunch. Republic is a well-armed lamb contesting the vote." This remark is almost certainly a product of internet fantasy. Differing versions of it have appeared, and Franklin probably didn't say it. All the same, it sounds like something Franklin would have said, and it makes a good point regardless of who deserves the credit for the remark.

In a democracy, anything goes as long as it receives anything over fifty percent of the vote. For example, in a democracy it is conceivable that husbands could legally kill annoying wives, wives could legally kill annoying husbands, parents could legally kill annoying children, and anyone could legally kill any other annoying person as long as at least 50.000001% of the people voted for it. But this would be a violation of the right to life –

something that a good government is supposed to defend. Democracy is no guarantee of good government. In a democracy is it possible that anyone could legally seize anyone else's property as long as at least 50.000001% of the people voted for it. But this would be a violation of the right to property – something that a good government is supposed to defend. Democracy is no guarantee of good government. In a democracy it would be legally permissible for one person to imprison and enslave another person as long as at least 50.000001% of the people voted for it. But this would be a violation of the right to liberty – something that a good government is supposed to defend. That's right, democracy is no guarantee of good government.

Our friend Lord Acton, mentioned in the Second Chapter of this book, wrote, "The one pervading evil of democracy is the tyranny of the majority, or rather of that party, not always the majority, that succeeds, by force or fraud, in carrying elections." This is the problem with democracies – or as many Founders called them, "mobocracies." They enshrine the fleeting will of any mere majority no matter how temporary or evil that opinion may be. They are inherently unstable and self-destructive. They are unstable because there are no consistent and enduring standards. Polygamy may be illegal yesterday, legal today, and illegal tomorrow. Abortion may be illegal yesterday, legal today, and illegal tomorrow. Same-sex marriage may be illegal yesterday, legal today, and illegal tomorrow. Private property may be illegal yesterday, legal today, and illegal tomorrow. Owning personal weapons may be illegal yesterday, legal today, and illegal tomorrow. We could go on, but I think you get the message. Democracies are inherently unstable and do not provide a proper foundation for the survival of a secure and successful society.

Democracies also are invariably self-destructive. At some point the slothful freeloaders of the society realize that they can vote themselves control over the wealth of the conscientious workers if they can get just 50+% of the voters to go along with them. When this happens the productive people get taxed more and more in order to support the unproductive. Sooner or later, the productive realize that it is pointless to create more wealth than they need to support themselves, they stop working hard, the economy fails, and the nation falls. As the author of the Declaration wrote elsewhere, "The democracy will cease to exist when you take away from those who are willing to work and give to those who would not."

So, what was the Founders' solution? A republic. In a republic the consent of the governed manifests itself through a process of representative government, but technically the people are not the ultimate authority. The law is. This principle has been called *Lex, Rex*, or "the law is king." In a republic the law must be obeyed even if it is inconsistent with the will of the majority. For example, there have been times in American history when a presidential candidate lost the popular vote (that is, more people voted for the other guy) but won the election because the laws pertaining to the Electoral College worked in his favor. The majority did not rule. The law did. *Lex, Rex*.

The people may change the law, but these changes must be consistent with the principles of some Supreme Law (like Holy Scripture or the Constitution), and they must be accomplished through the laborious machine of representative government. Changes in the law will take time, and sometimes they won't be permitted at all because the change – no matter how popular – will contradict a fundamental principle expressed in the Supreme Law. Accordingly, republics tend to be much more stable than democracies. This is no guarantee of success, but then, there are no guarantees of success. Still, a republic is a much better long-term bet than a democracy.

To summarize, "the consent of the governed" is expressed through the process of representative government; it is moderated by the principle of the rule of law (*Lex, Rex*) not the rule of the majority; and it is accomplished over time.

... That whenever any Form of Government becomes destructive of these ends, it is the Right of the People to alter or to abolish it, and to institute new Government....

Here is the cornerstone of our declaration of independence – the reason why we were entitled to legitimately separate ourselves from Great Britain. The government of Great Britain had become "destructive" of its most solemn and sacred responsibility. As was summarized earlier, "Governments are instituted among Men" "to secure these rights" "that ... are endowed by their Creator...." This is the foremost responsibility of any government; and if a government fails to do this, or actively works against this, it is illegitimate and deserves to be altered or abolished. The Founders actually proclaimed that "it is the *Right* of the People to alter or to abolish it, and to institute new Government...." (Emphasis added.) Obviously, this is one of those other rights alluded to when the Declaration states "among these" rights.

When a government fails in its ultimate responsibility to secure the people's rights – or worse, to actually endanger or abrogate them – the people are lawfully and morally entitled to alter or abolish that government. By what means? By any means necessary, including violence. Thomas Jefferson, the man who understood the principles of the Declaration better than any other, once wrote, "I hold it that a little rebellion now and then is a good thing and as necessary in the political world as storms in the physical." He also believed, "The tree of liberty must be refreshed from time to time with the blood of patriots and tyrants." It is the God-given right of the people to alter or abolish an illegitimate government – peacefully or otherwise.

This nation and its government were founded on the belief that the people are entitled to the exercise of their fundamental rights. If the government fails to defend these rights – and, especially, if the government betrays the people and violates these rights – the people are entitled to change or destroy that government and establish a new one. This principle applies if the offending government is in London, a state capital, or Washington, D.C.

... laying its foundation on such principles and organizing its powers in such form, as to them shall seem most likely to effect their Safety and Happiness.

Superficially, this statement seems to be an endorsement of the very democratic principles which we said the Founders did not support. It appears that the Declaration is adopting the view that "it is the Right of the People" "to institute [a] new Government" that "shall seem most likely to effect their Safety and Happiness." Yes, but the type of government that will be "most likely to effect their Safety and Happiness" is a republic that is fully committed to securing those rights which were endowed by their Creator. Anything other than this, ultimately, will fail in accomplishing "their Safety and Happiness."

*   *   *

Before we proceed to discuss the political paradigm of "up-down," we need to address one other important issue embedded in the text of the Declaration which was quoted above. As we said earlier, the primary responsibility of government is the protection of the rights endowed to the people by their Creator. When the Declaration began to enumerate these rights, it said that "among" these are life, liberty, and the pursuit of happiness. It later included the right of the people to alter or abolish an illegitimate government – what has been called the

"Right of Rebellion." The question remains, "What are the other rights?" Many are specifically mentioned in the Constitution and its amendments. Several others, however, have wormed their way into the modern political conversation. It has, in fact, become commonplace for the advocates of any desire to describe their fantasy as a "right" in the hope that it will get a free pass and become canon. Despite this, many of these do not possess the credentials of legitimacy.

This is not the place for a comprehensive discussion of true or legitimate rights; but we must point out an important criterion to be used in determining the legitimacy of a claim to "righthood." Please recall that the Declaration states that the rights of man are "endowed by their Creator." Accordingly, all true rights must consist of only those behaviors and activities which are consistent with the will and pleasure of God. A right is something which God gives us permission to do. In other words, if someone claims that something is a "right", but that "something" is contrary to the Founder's understanding of the will of God, it is not a right. Obviously, He is not going to give us permission to do something that He finds offensive. Let us look at a couple of contemporary claims to "righthood" which do not stand the test.

Since January, 1973, it has been legal for women in the United States to obtain abortions. This was made possible by the United States Supreme Court's ruling in *Roe v. Wade*. In brief, the Court ruled that women have a "right" to an abortion. "Based on what?" we might ask.

Well, some say the right to privacy, or to liberty, or to do what one wants with one's own body. But what is the ultimate criterion for determining the difference between a "right" – which is legitimate and unalienable – and a mere desire – which may be quite perverse, illegitimate, and impermissible? The answer is: the will of God. Remember, the Declaration says that we are endowed by our *Creator* with rights. Rights come from God; and, surely, God will not give us the unalienable permission to do something which is against His will. Now, we may choose to do such a thing, but we do not have permission to do so. Accordingly, only those things which are consistent with the will and desires of God can be rights. Conversely, nothing can be a right which is inconsistent with the will and desires of God. Now, it is hard to imagine that the Judeo-Christian God of the Founders would find it acceptable to terminate the lives of the most innocent and helpless members of God's family merely because their existence is inconvenient. Accordingly, there is no right to abortion. The United States Supreme Court was clearly wrong on this matter.

Another contentious, contemporary issue is same-sex marriage. Some argue that homosexuals have a "right" to "marry." Again we must ask, "Based on what?" They argue that if heterosexuals are allowed to do something, then homosexuals should also be allowed to do the same thing based on the "equal protection" clause of the Fourteenth Amendment. Well, that sounds like a conclusive argument until we remember that the **only** criterion for determining whether a behavior can be considered a "right" is "the will and desires of God." The verdict, therefore, is clear. It doesn't matter whether one is talking about Jehovah or Allah (which the Founders wouldn't) – it doesn't matter whether you turn to the Old Testament, the New Testament, or the Koran (which the Founders wouldn't) – homosexual conduct is an "abomination" in the eyes of God. Accordingly, there is no right to homosexual marriage. Any court that rules otherwise is clearly wrong.

This same criterion can be used to define the limits of rights. No responsible theory of rights has ever claimed that the exercise of these rights was unrestricted. For example, in 1878 the United States Supreme Court upheld the conviction of George Reynolds for bigamy. As a member of the Church of Jesus Christ of Latter-day Saints, Reynolds argued that it was his right (under the First Amendment) and his duty (as a Mormon) to marry more than one wife. The Court ruled that some practices are simply too contrary to the general values of the society to be protected and permitted. (*Reynolds v. United States*) Human sacrifices would be another example. Similarly, the First Amendment protection of free speech does not allow an individual to say anything he desires. In *Schenck v. United States* in 1919, Justice Oliver Wendell Holmes, Jr., argued that, "The most stringent protection of free speech would not protect a man in falsely shouting fire in a theatre and causing a panic." We also agree that one is not free to slander another; that is, to tell malicious lies.

Rights are not unlimited, but how can we know when someone has gone too far? Where do we draw the line that divides permissible exercise from impermissible abuse? Again, the criteria are the will and desires of God. Just as an act which is against the will of God cannot be legitimately considered a right, neither can the exercise of a right be considered legitimate if it results in conduct which is displeasing to God. A good example of a practice which has been wrongly ruled to be a legitimate exercise of the "right of free expression" (Gee, I missed that one in the Constitution) is pornography. Surely, the shameful exploitation of God's children in order to satisfy the prurient interests of others cannot be pleasing to God. Accordingly, pornography is not a protected aspect of free speech.

*   *   *

The time has come to define the politics of "Ascendancy" and to introduce the "Up–Down" political paradigm. As was noted earlier, the political philosophy of "Ascendancy" is mission-oriented. At its heart is the answer to this question: What is the proper purpose of government? Our examination of the second paragraph of the Declaration of Independence reveals that, "Governments are instituted among Men" "to secure these rights" "that ... are endowed by their Creator...." Hence, the highest calling and objective of government – and those who administer it – is to secure and preserve the unalienable rights of the people, the most sacred of which are life, property, and liberty. The primary and pre-eminent mission of government – at all levels – is to max-imize the free exercise of the people's rights. The primary and preeminent responsibility of all those who serve in government – at all levels – is to maximize the free exer-cise of the people's rights. The failure of a government official in accomplishing this goal is a demonstration of incompetence and grounds for immediate dismissal. Should a government official actively work against this goal, he is assailing the highest law of the land, and, ac-cordingly, is guilty of treason. When a government fails to accomplish this goal, or actively works against it, that government has become illegitimate, and the people are authorized to alter or abolish it.

The goal of Ascendancy is to forever strive to create an environment in which the people may enjoy the free exercise of their God-given rights – that is, behaviors consistent with the will and pleasure of God. If a nation achieves this noble objective, it is "ascendant." If a nation is actively progressing toward this objective, it is "ascend-ing." If a nation is losing the free exercise of these God-given rights, it is "decaying." If a nation is substantially deprived of the free exercise of these God-given rights, it is "decadent."

Now, consider the "Up – Down" scale shown below. Governments can be rated according to how well they are promoting, protecting, and preserving the rights of the people. Governments which do an excellent job of this will receive a higher grade than those which do not. Obviously, the goal is to get the highest grade possible.

Ascendant

10

9

8

7

6

5

4

3

2

1

Decadent

It is not only important to consider how well a government is doing at present, but it also is important to look for trends by comparing its current grade with past grades. This historic "report card" will give the citizens of a nation an important indicator as to how well their government officials are doing in honoring their most important responsibility. It also will give current government officials a clear notion about their present mission – whether it is to preserve a good situation or to promote a better one. Remember, the goal is to stay high on the scale or to move higher.

Regarding the United States, it could reasonably be argued that we probably earned a grade of "7" or "8" early in our national life. That grade would have been higher had we not permitted the practice of slavery and had we granted equal rights to women. Still, this was an excellent score by historic standards. Currently, we would be hard-pressed to justify a "6." Granted, the assignment of such numerical values is a bit subjective – and different evaluators might assign different numbers – but there can be no argument that Americans are much less free to enjoy their basic and true rights now than they were earlier in our history. Accordingly, we have been "decaying," and the foremost responsibility of our government administrators (executives, legislators, and jurists) is to reverse this trend and become "ascendant."

I am sure that there are those who would contest the statement above that, "there can be no argument that Americans are much less free to enjoy their basic and true rights now than they were earlier in our history." These critics would argue that more, not fewer, Americans are enjoying such freedoms as the freedom from economic want (due to labor laws and entitlement programs), the freedom to choose what to do with their bodies (legalized abortion), the freedom to express themselves (pornography), the freedom to love (same-sex "marriage"), etc. Keep in mind, however, that "freedoms" and "rights" are not synonymous. "Rights" refer to those God-given core liberties which are most fundamental to the pursuit of true happiness. All of the "freedoms" mentioned above are not only dubious "accomplishments," they also have been achieved at the expense of some core right or at the expense of some principle of rights. The "freedom from economic want" was accomplished at the expense of another person's property rights and liberties. (For example, my property was confiscated in order to redistribute to another, or my freedom to dispose of my labor was infringed by labor laws.) The "freedom to choose" what to do with one's own body is accomplished at the expense of another's right to life. The freedoms to express oneself pornographically or to romantically love indiscriminately are accomplished by violating the will and pleasure of the very Creator who gave us these rights. "Maximizing freedoms" and "maximizing rights" are not one and the same thing. Maximizing rights will generally work to strengthen a nation. Maximizing freedoms will tear it asunder.

Cardinal, categorical, and conditional.

At this point I would like to introduce another concept pertaining to the issue of rights. In Jefferson's early, but subsequently edited, version of the Declaration, he referred to "inherent and unalienable rights." It is not clear whether he intended to imply that all true rights share these two characteristics (that is, being both inherent *and* unalienable) or whether he was referring to two classes of rights (that is, some that are inherent and some that are unalienable). I would argue that our Holy Trinity of Rights – life, property, and liberty – in fact consist of two distinct classes of rights. "Life" and "property" are categorical whereas "liberty" is cardinal.

The right of "Liberty" is definitely in a class by itself. Liberty is the "enabling right." It is the right which gives wings to the other rights. "Life" and "property" are categorical rights in that these are the areas, or categories, where liberty may be legitimately exercised. But without the liberty to exercise one's rights, the possession of those rights is essentially worthless. What value is my life if I am not at liberty to make decisions as to how it should be lived? What value is my property if I am not at liberty to make decisions at to how it should be used? Accordingly, liberty is cardinal. It is of preeminent importance. It is the breath of life that invigorates and empowers the other rights. It is the life blood of a meaningful existence. Liberty is the most critical right. It also is the most misunderstood and definitely the most dangerous to indulge. In order to clear up the misunderstanding and minimize the danger, it will be necessary to spend a little time distinguishing "liberty" from "freedom."

In brief, "freedom" is unlimited and unrestricted. Freedom is undisciplined. "Liberty" is freedom once it has been limited and restricted. "Liberty", accordingly, is permitted and conditional. It is disciplined. During the time I served in the United States Marines, I was essentially the property of the Corps. I was at its disposal twenty-four hours a day, seven days a week. My superiors would occasionally grant me permission to leave the base and experience some recreation and relaxation, as long as I observed a code of conduct and returned to base by a designated hour. This time off was permitted and conditional and was called, "Liberty."

The same is true of our rights as citizens. We are *permitted* to enjoy certain liberties as long as we observe certain *conditions*. "Liberty" does not allow us to do things which have not been permitted. For example, even though I have "religious liberty," I am not permitted to kill someone, call it human sacrifice, and claim it as a right. That particular exercise of freedom crosses a line – specifically, depriving another of the categorical right to life – and is not permitted. "Liberty" also does not allow us to do things which exist outside the boundaries of certain conditions. For example, even though I have the liberty to express myself, I may not yell "Fire!" in a crowded theater causing a panic when there is no fire. That violates one of the conditions of free speech. The panic induced by yelling "Fire!" could negatively impact other persons' lives and property while accomplishing no counterbalancing good.

"Freedom" is unrestricted and unconditional. Accordingly, freedom is irresponsible because it is not constrained by any obligation to another person's interests and rights. Freedom is the objective of anarchists. It results in violent, abusive, and oppressive chaos; which, in turn, results in the establishment of a violent, abusive, and oppressive tyranny in order to restore order and safety.

"Liberty," on the other hand, is responsible freedom. It recognizes the rights of everyone. It is only permitted among those who acknowledge and accept certain minimal but necessary conditions – conditions usually designed to insure that the rights of all are honored.

The categorical rights of life and property exist and are functional from conception, whereas the right of liberty exists at conception but should not become functional until certain minimal personal development takes place. Think of it this way: all of the systems of the body are present at birth, but not all of the systems (like the reproductive system) are functional from birth. There is a certain amount of physical, intellectual, and emotional development which should take place before reproduction is possible. The same is true of liberty. It is dangerous to entrust liberties to those who are not prepared to use them. It also is dangerous to say what I just said, because it can be used by tyrants as an excuse to deprive the "unprepared" of their liberties. I offer no apologies nor equivocations, just an admission that life often is messy – and dangerous.

"Okay," you may be thinking, "you said 'the rights of life and property exist and are functional from conception', but then you said that although the right of liberty exists at conception, it should not be functional until later. But, what good are these rights if I don't have the liberty to use them? You yourself said, 'What value is my life if I am not at liberty to make decisions as to how it should be lived? What value is my property if I am not at liberty to make decisions at to how it should be used?'"

Excellent question! Glad to see that you were paying attention.

The categorical rights of life and property are inherent and unalienable. They exist at conception and cannot be taken away legitimately. However, during the early stages of life these rights are merely "defensive" in nature. What does that mean? No one's rights to life and property can be *denied* at any age unless that person has committed a serious violation of the "sacred covenant" mentioned earlier – something that is not likely among newborns or young children. On the other hand, the liberty to use these rights willfully does not kick in until later – after the person is capable of understanding and honoring the conditions under which the exercise of liberties may be permitted. In short, a person's rights must always be defended (the "defensive" aspect mentioned above), but they may not always be exercised. For example, let us assume a proud father signs over the deed to his speedy sports car to his newborn son. The "defensive" aspect of the infant's property rights applies immediately. No one can deprive the child of his property, but neither will the child be permitted the liberty to use his property until years later when he can reasonably be expected to do so responsibly. His rights are defended (the "defensive" aspect of the right), but he may not yet have the liberty to exercise them himself.

So, what preconditions must exist before the right of liberty may be exercised? I would argue that a good starter list would necessarily include knowledge, wisdom, morals, and self-control.

Knowledge. Knowledge consists of the information a person has learned and retained. It is an essential prerequisite for the exercise of liberty. Without a minimal base of relevant knowledge, liberty cannot be exercised constructively and responsibly. Let us use the example of driving a car. I may be a sublimely wonderful person in all other respects, but if I do not possess a basic knowledge consisting of such things as how to operate an automobile, the rules of the road, and some basic maintenance skills, it would be very unwise to trust me with the keys to the car. I simply do not know enough to keep from causing trouble, or worse. Liberty should not be permitted to those who do not have sufficient knowledge to use that liberty responsibly.

Wisdom. "Knowledge" is what you know. "Wisdom" is the sense to use what you know prudently, constructively, and responsibly. "Knowledge" is the awareness that a tomato is a fruit, not a vegetable. "Wisdom" is knowing better than to put it in a fruit salad. Wisdom is also a prerequisite for exercising liberty. Let us continue with our automobile example in order to illustrate this point. Let's say I have acquired all the basic knowledge about cars that was listed above. In fact, let's say that I am a master mechanic, a skilled driver, and have memorized all the the thousands of vehicular laws that pertain to operating an automobile. But let's also say that I don't have enough sense to keep from driving one hundred miles an hour past an elementary school at dismissal time on a narrow, winding, residential road during a drenching rain storm. I've got the knowledge, but I clearly don't have the judgment – wisdom – to use that knowledge responsibly. I must not be allowed the liberty of driving. Liberty should not be permitted to those who do not have sufficient wisdom to use that liberty responsibly.

Morality. "Morality" pertains to the ability to discern good and bad behavior. This, too, is a prerequisite for liberty. A person could be very knowledgable, aware of how to use this knowledge wisely, but lacking the scruples to do so. He may choose to use his knowledge and wisdom for destructive purposes – like a master criminal or politician, but then I repeat myself. Continuing with our automobile analogy, suppose a person were very knowledgable about cars, prudent and skillful in the application of this knowledge, but used these talents to serve as a get-away driver for bank robbers or to deliver car bombs for terrorists. He's got the knowledge and wisdom but not the morals to use that knowledge and wisdom responsibly. Liberty should not be permitted to those who do not have sufficient morals to use that liberty responsibly.

Self-control. As its name suggests, "self-control" is the ability to discipline or control oneself. The self-controlled person will make himself do the proper thing. He does not require the direction of someone else to make him do the proper thing. This is another essential prerequisite for liberty. A person could be knowledgable, wise, moral, and yet lack the self-discipline to make him abide by his knowledge, wisdom, and morality. Suppose a person were very knowledgable about automobiles, wise enough to know how to use that knowledge carefully, and moral enough to know better than to use that knowledge for evil purposes, but lacked the self-control to actually drive accordingly. He still drove one hundred miles an hour past an elementary school on a winding, narrow, residential road at dismissal time during a drenching rain storm just because it seemed like too much fun to resist. He's got the knowledge as well as the wisdom and morals to use that knowledge responsibly, but he just can't make himself do it. Liberty should not be permitted to those who do not have sufficient self-control to use that liberty responsibly.

*   *   *

Now that we have made this necessary detour to explore the nature of our cardinal and categorical rights – and the conditions which apply to their exercise – let's return to the practical application of all this. As we said earlier, the primary and preeminent mission of government – at all levels – is to maximize the free exercise of the people's rights. Governments which do this well are "ascendant." Those which are improving at this are "ascending." Those which are moving away from accomplishing this mission (like the modern-day United States) are "decaying." Those which do a poor job at accomplishing this are "decadent." Both government officials and the citizenry must constantly assess the progress of their own nation in terms of accomplishing this all-important mission. This on-going assessment is necessary to determine whether the present mission is to preserve a good situation or to promote a better one. Remember, the goal is to stay high on the Up-Down Scale or to move higher.

It should be emphasized at this point that whereas the *ultimate* objective of every nation should be to become Ascendent, this cannot be the *immediate* goal of every nation. Not all are prepared to move directly to the Ascendent position. I made a reference earlier in the chapter to "immature" societies. Immature societies, like immature individuals, cannot be trusted with significant liberties. A five-year-old, for example, should not be trusted with the keys to the car, a bottle of booze, a cigarette lighter, the privilege of voting, nor a loaded handgun. The reason is obvious – or as Jefferson might put it, "self evident." A five-year-old simply has not yet attained the attributes necessary to be entrusted with these liberties without a high probability of abuse taking place. The same is true of many – perhaps most – societies in the world. They simply have not yet attained the attributes necessary to be entrusted with the same liberties that can be entrusted to others. They will use them imprudently and cause more harm than good. So, what are these critical social attributes? The same ones we mentioned above: knowledge, wisdom, morals, and self-control.

Whereas the *ultimate* objective of government – at all levels – is to maximize the free exercise of the people's rights, the *immediate* objective of immature societies should be to defend the people's rights of life and property and to prepare the people for the liberty of exercising these rights. This single statement provides the basis for a powerful condemnation of American foreign policy in many areas of the world. We seem convinced that our job is to make everyone a "Little America" when, clearly, most of these nations are simply not prepared to become us. Instead of working, funding, and bleeding to create democratic republics, we should be willing to assist the efforts of other nations to gain the knowledge, wisdom, morals, and self-control necessary to ascend the Up-Down Scale. The governments of immature societies should be working to do the same thing.

*   *   *

Well, this ought to give the reader something new to think about. The problem, however, is that we do not easily give up old habits. Even though the reader has been given the insights necessary to arise, he is likely already falling back into old thoughts about the perilous paradigm. "But," he wonders desperately, "just how big should the government be?"

No bigger than it needs to be, but this is not a constant. According to the "First and Second Laws of Political History" discussed in Chapter Two, government strongly tends to become the favorite tool of tyrannical minorities in abusing the general populace for their selfish purposes. The amassing of such power as we typically find in government attracts the worst of the worst of us and will almost inevitably be turned to serve their wicked purposes. It is always in our best interest to keep government as small as possible. Still, we did say that governments tend to amass power, and we did argue that "power" is the ability to get something done. Some societies – especially immature ones and those facing a profound external or internal threat – simply need more power than others in order to advance and protect their legitimate interests. As much as I hate to say it, it is sometimes necessary for governments to increase in power – or to delay the divestment of power – in order to deal with a crisis or imperative challenge. We have seen this in our own history. General Washington did not observe the same principles in fighting for a republic that President Washington observed in establishing it. But regardless of the presence or absence of crisis, the highest calling of government will always be "to secure these rights" with which we "are endowed by [our] Creator."

Ultimately, only the people can keep the government on track. It is the people's responsibility to remain ever vigilant in the defense of their rights, ever watchful for abuse within their government, and ever ready to employ the ballot or the bullet in the defense of their rights.

We have failed to do this. We have allowed the very government that was formed to "secure these rights" to become "destructive of these ends." Accordingly, the time has come for us either to accept the tyranny of our government or "to alter or to abolish it." The time has come for "we the people" to arise and begin the second American Revolution.

Like the first American Revolution, the second – AR2 – will be fought against an oppressor who denies the people the exercise of the rights endowed to them by their Creator. Unlike the first American Revolution, the second American Revolution will not be fought against a foreign oppressor but against a domestic one. Unlike the first Revolution, the second may well begin in the West – perhaps even in California, as strange as that may sound. Before long, it will be embraced by others and become nationwide. Like the first Revolution, it is the sincere hope of today's "rebels" that the goals of this second Revolution can be achieved peacefully; but that hope was not realized by the rebels of the 1770s, and it may not be realized this time either. Like the first Revolution, the second will be fought against a tyrannical empire, but one that has no flag and is not so easily recognizable as before. This evil empire consists of a cartel of political and economic interests – both domestic and international – which conspire and cooperate to oppress the masses for their own advantage. (See the First Law of Political History.) This second revolution will be vigorously, probably violently, opposed by those who have a vested interest in the dysfunctional, diseased system they have created. Among these opponents of liberty's cause are the leaders of the Republican and Democratic Party Machines, the central bankers, and the leaders of large business and labor organizations. Please note: laborers and the owners of small and medium businesses will be benefitted greatly by AR2. They are not the enemy. They are those for whom we fight. However, the *leaders* of large political, economic, business, and labor organizations often have an agenda which does not favor those beneath them in the organizational chart. Remember: the accumulation of great power tends to attract the worst of the worst of us: those who are very willing to exploit their power in order to oppress others. (See the Second Law of Political History.) Like the first American Revolution, the goal of the second is to return control over a person's life to that person. Like the first American Revolution, the second will require time and much sacrifice to accomplish, for – like the first time – we are fighting against the most powerful empire on earth. Unlike the first American Revolution, the second will not likely be led by military generals but by state governors and county sheriffs. These, however, will not be the unprincipled political calculators and bureaucratic administrators of today. These will be a new breed of bold, dynamic, and courageous leaders who will hold high the banner of liberty and charge valiantly into the future.

Like the first American Revolution, we the people will emerge victorious.

In the next section we will discuss Eight Elements which offer the best chance for the second American Revolution to accomplish its objectives without a resort to violence.

God help us if we fail.

PART TWO

THE EIGHT ELEMENTS OF THE REVOLUTION

CHAPTER SEVEN

TIME TO CRASH THE PARTY; NO PARTY AFFILIATION

Millions of Americans have experienced the thrill and terror of starting their own businesses. Frequently the motivation for such an endeavor is to build "a better mousetrap." Someone told Mom that her cookies and cakes were so good that she ought to open a bakery. Someone admires Dad's woodworking skills and urges him to start a carpentry shop. A faithful employee keeps suggesting ways to improve the business to the boss, but the boss keeps brushing him off. Finally, the employee decides to go out on his own and prove himself right. At first the goal of these mom-and-pop startups is quality. The entrepreneur believes he has a better idea and wants to share it with the world. At some point, however, this shining idealism is tarnished, and more mundane objectives take over. "I'm overworked. I have no time for my family. Life has become drudgery. I need to make more money. I must expand my operation." Mom starts using preservatives and less expensive ingredients. Dad starts using screws and nails instead of tongue and groove. The former employee starts acting more and more like his former employer. Compromises are made. Principles are sacrificed. Instead of selling the best, we sell-out to be the best. It becomes about winning, instead of that for which you seek to win. The little shop that made it right abandons its ideals to become the mega-chain that made the most.

This isn't a trait of business. It is a trait of human nature. It manifests itself in manifold areas – including, and perhaps especially, in politics.

When the sun rose over New York City on the morning of April 30, 1789, it would soon illuminate a remarkable event. The first President of the United States under the Constitution would be inaugurated. In more ways than one, a new day had dawned.

George Washington had been the only Commander of the Continental Army during the eight years of the Revolution. He accomplished the impossible. He defeated the greatest empire on earth with a ragtag band of ill-trained and poorly-supplied troops. In 1787 Washington was chosen to be the President of the Constitutional Convention. He accomplished the impossible. He oversaw the drafting of a profoundly wise and innovative plan of government that united thirteen proud, diverse, and divisive sovereign states into one grand union. Two years later Washington was unanimously selected by the Electoral College to lead this new nation. He accomplished the impossible. His wisdom and character provided the glue that held the often contradictory and contrary elements of a far-flung country together and gave it a sense of direction, identity, and mission that would propel it to greatness. He was the "indispensable man." It is too bad that modern-day fools have sought to dispense with him.

When George Washington became President, there were no political parties. Washington liked it that way, and he would have preferred that it stayed that way. Unfortunately, it didn't last long. In 1791 the Federalist Party emerged with Alexander Hamilton and John Adams as its leaders. The next year the Anti-Federalist, or Democratic-Republican Party, arose under the leadership of Thomas Jefferson. This was a development that greatly concerned Washington and threatened the unity of his administration. You see, all three of the men cited above were members of Washington's leadership team. Adams was Vice-President, Hamilton was Secretary of the Treasury, and Jefferson was Secretary of State. As the president of a republic, and not the king of a monarchy, Washington could not stop the rise of political parties, but he advised against them as earnestly as he could. In his farewell address, Washington warned of the "disorders and miseries" which could be expected from the development of a party system. He alerted us to the "common and continual mischiefs of the spirit of party...." This party spirit "kindles the animosity of one part against another, foments occasionally riot and insurrection." He sagely advised that it is "the interest and duty of a wise people to discourage and restrain it." Sadly, the indispensable wisdom of the indispensable man was dispensed with.

Washington was not alone in this judgment against parties. Thomas Paine, the pamphleteer of the American Revolution, is perhaps best known for the opening line of *The American Crisis*: "These are the times that try men's souls", first published in late 1776. This same luminary of the Great Rebellion also weighed in on the divisiveness of parties. "Let the names of Whig and Tory [the two major political viewpoints of Englishmen at the time] be extinct; and let none other be heard among us, than those of a good citizen, a resolute friend, and a virtuous supporter of the rights of mankind and of the free and independent states of America." More good advice that has been ignored.

Every modern-American has grown up in a country where the government has been dominated by two political parties. The experience has been so universal that it is hard to imagine it could be anything different. But we must imagine. In fact, we must dare to act and recreate.

Washington was right. The party system simply has caused too many "disorders and miseries." It started out nobly – perhaps – but its genetic code is loaded with so many noxious elements that it is virtually impossible for it to grow without developing some terrible deformity or disease. Like the mom-and-pop companies mentioned above, a party often starts off with lofty ideals, but then the "business" of politics takes over, and the goal shifts from doing what is right to doing what will win. The interests of the party – and especially of those who run the party machine – take precedence over the interests of the people. The goal isn't to serve the masses. The goal is to hoodwink the masses into supporting "our" side long enough so that the fat cats who run the machine can fleece them. And lest the reader should think that I have gone 'round the bend into the dark shadows of wacky, conspiratorial theorists, consider this. I personally listened to a candidate for state party chairman of one of the "Big Two" parties in one of the biggest states in the Union as he campaigned for votes at a county central committee meeting. Did he speak of lofty ideals or the rectitude of their party's platform? Not one word. What he did talk about was the need to get more money and more votes. His plan for doing this was essentially to become more like the "other guys" because they were doing such a stellar job of humiliating his old, grand party at the polls. Apparently, the strategy is, "If you can't beat 'em, join 'em – just keep it a secret." By the way, this candidate won election handily.

Let us look at a few of the glaring problems associated with party politics and the party system. First of all, keep in mind that the "Spirit of the Party" is the "Spirit of the Part." Party politics isn't about all of us, it's about some of us. It is divisive, not unifying. It is exclusive, not inclusive. It is adversarial, not amicable. It is institutionalized and legalized warfare, and the battleground is our land, our lives, and our livelihood. It fosters and encourages an "us versus them" attitude. Accordingly, party politics usually devolves into "attack ads" and a laser-like focus on emphasizing differences. A happy, peaceful, and prosperous society, however, requires a healthy measure of unity and agreement. That's just not on the menu of "Party Politics." The party politician needs an enemy and a war. We the people need friends and peace.

In a system where party politics prevail, the party machine becomes the primary path to public office. The party machine is where the action is if you are interested in holding such an office. If you hope to be a successful candidate, you are going to have to get your ticket punched by those who run the machine. Unless you happen to be a celebrity, you will have to pay your dues by serving the party and subordinating your interests to the interests of the party until the party believes you could be useful for accomplishing its purposes. If you do happen to be a celebrity, you can often bypass the party's "time in grade" requirements for being a candidate, but you still will likely be expected to subordinate your interests to those of the machine. Now, remember that in Chapter Two it was pointed out that government concentrates a great deal of power in conveniently compact locations. Accordingly, it was argued that government service "will attract the worst of the worst of us – the most selfish of the selfish – like a steaming pile of manure attracts all manner of vile insects." So, if the power of government attracts the worst of us like manure attracts bugs, and if the party machine provides the primary path to government office, I guess that we can conclude that party headquarters is the first steaming pile this side of the capital. As such, party headquarters often functions as a clearing house for scoundrels. Think of all the good that would come if we simply mucked the barn and eliminated these dens of iniquity.

As the pathway to power, the party machines not only attract those who crave that power, they also become lucrative targets of opportunity for those who want to influence the use of that power. The work of many special interest groups has been made much easier by the party system. Instead of having to confront hundreds of federal legislators and thousands of state law-makers in unending one-to-one encounters, a few well-placed contacts at party headquarters will suffice. The party mechanics will carry the ball for them, and woe be unto any person of conscience who entertains ideas of resistance. Can you spell "One and done"? The party system often opens the door to special interests while slamming it in the face of the general welfare.

Since the party machine paves the pathway to power, the party machine, itself, becomes an organism of unspeakable power. You want power? Pay homage to the Machine. You want to influence the use of that power? Pay the Machine. This accumulation of political and economic might not only gives the party machines power over who may run for office, who will retain office, and who gets to influence those in office; it also gives the machines power over us because they – not we – decide who will be our "representatives." They also dictate the agenda that will be pursued. We the people are left to wonder about and wait for the candidates and causes which the Machine decides are best for us.

Certain grass-roots groups have arisen to counter the power of the Machines. A prominent one that surged into the spotlight around 2008 sought to capture and reform the Republican Party. Nice thought. Bad plan. They met with some initial success, but have been fading recently. Why? Like I said, "Nice thought. Bad plan." It is crucial that grass-roots groups arise, but not so they can become "them." They should and must be the antithesis of party politics, not the next stage in its evolution. I'm sure that many grass-rooters thought, "Why reinvent the wheel? Let's just take over the party that seems closest to our ideals." There is some superficial appeal to this idea; unless, of course, the wheel is square. In that case, it might be far more productive to start over from scratch than to attempt to repair the broken wheel. Additionally, the grass-rooters have proved to be no match for the machinations of the veteran party machinists. These machinists are too good at what they do. They will always beat you if you play their game. So, don't play their game. Leave the stadium, find a sandlot somewhere, and play a game that is more interesting to we the people.

Another problem with a system of party politics is that it is a great facilitator of voter fraud – which has become rampant in modern America. I volunteered to assist a non-partisan organization which works to minimize voter fraud. Among other things, I received training to assist the county office which maintains the records of eligible voters. I, and others, were trained to look for instances where a voter might be registered more than once – whether by accident or design. We were taught to flag such entries as "John Doe, born 1/13/85" and "John L. Doe, born 1/13/85" where both lived at the same address. Such multiple entries could allow one person to cast more than one vote. This is especially likely in "vote by mail" which is becoming more prevalent. Frankly, I wondered if I would be able to find any suspected culprits. I was shocked to see that, by the time I finished processing my first stack of records, nearly one-third of the entries were "suspicious." That creates a huge potential for voter fraud; but the ability to turn that potential into a reality is maximized in a party system where a structure exists to organize the fraud and profit from it.

Significant voter fraud is unlikely to develop apart from a system that has longevity – and parties, like vampires, live a long time. Suppose we had no parties, and each candidate ran on his personal merits. Even if a candidate were inclined to benefit from voter fraud, he would have to invest in a long-term, expensive, illegal, and dangerous effort to amass enough fraudulent votes to sway an election. Should he actually accomplish this, either time or the voters would likely have caught up with him, and he would either retire to the farm or buy one. Parties, however, live long enough to make systematic fraud productive and worth the risk. "Candidate A" may retire or die, but "Candidate B" from the same party will be waiting in the wings. Neither will have the time to build his own cadre of fraudulent voters, but both will be able to cash in on the on-going efforts of the party.

Another dysfunctional aspect of party politics is the tendency to devolve into Pavlovian responses to political proposals. Ivan Pavlov was a Russian physiologist who did a great deal of research on the reflex systems of the body. In what was perhaps his best known experiment, Pavlov would ring a bell before feeding his dogs. Eventually, the dogs associated the ringing of the bell with being fed, and they would actually start to salivate before the food arrived. Similarly, many modern politicians react reflexively to who is proposing or perpetrating a course of action. They are more concerned with the party affiliation of the author of some proposal than with the merits of the proposition. For example, if a Republican president (Bush) engages in massive deficit spending, Republicans argue that it is reasonable while Democrats find it irresponsible. If a Democratic president (Obama) engages in massive deficit spending, Democrats argue that it is reasonable while Republicans find it irresponsible. Good dog! Now, wipe your chin. In such a system, the merits of a plan often have little to do with the acceptability of a plan. The overriding issue is, "Who will get the credit and how many donations and votes can we garner?" Promoting the general welfare often has little to do with political strategizing between the parties. Politics becomes a sectarian chess match where each side drools over the prospect of ravaging the other side's queen. The political system degenerates into unending head-butting where the politicians get the publicity (along with the payroll, perks, and pensions) while we the people get the migraines. The time has come for we the people to send these slobbering hounds to the kennel and lock them up until they know how to behave in civil society.

So, what is the alternative? No party affiliation – or better yet, no parties at all.

"My goodness!", the reader may be thinking. "How could that possibly work?" It's easier than you think, and the only reason it doesn't seem simple is because we, like Pavlov's dogs and party politicians, have been conditioned to think in terms of party politics. We have been trained to think and act "inside boxes" that were created by others in order to control our thoughts and actions. Such boxes, however, are no places for a free people, and it is high time for us to bust out of them.

The simple fact is, we don't need parties. Suppose we outlawed the use of such words as "Democrat," "Republican," "right," "left," "liberal," "conservative," or any other descriptive group title. What would candidates talk about? They would talk about the values and principles they believe in and what they would do if elected. Good! That's exactly what they should be talking about and exactly how we voters should be making our decisions. Every campaign would be a grass-roots campaign that focuses on issues, principles, and actions instead of a party moniker.

The reader may be thinking, "Well, that might work at the local level, but you need an organization to carry out a campaign at the state and national level." Do we? I would suggest that you are still a "box-dweller" and need to free your mind. Think about this. Our greatest leaders emerged during a time in our history when political parties did not exist or were in their infancy. George Washington, John Adams, Thomas Jefferson, Benjamin Franklin, Alexander Hamilton, John Hancock, Patrick Henry, Samuel Adams, George Mason, John Jay, James Madison, etc., all rose to prominence and power without the aid of radio, television, the social media, celebrity endorsements, and with precious little – or no – help from party machines. I suspect it is no coincidence that the Golden Age of American Statesmen corresponds with a time when political parties were absent or at their weakest. In the absence of party machines, the cream will rise to the top. In a system dominated by party politics, the crumbs will rise to the top.

CHAPTER EIGHT

BECAUSE THEY CAN; REAL TAX REFORM

Why do politicians keep raising our taxes? Because they can. But, what if they couldn't? The only way Americans are going to see meaningful and lasting tax relief is to force the politicians to sit on their hands and then nail their thighs to the chair. Well, maybe that metaphor is a bit graphic, but you get the message. If we allow the politicians any wiggle room, they are going to wiggle. That's what worms do.

Consider the following: Accounts Receivable Tax, Building Permit Tax, Cigarette Tax, Corporate Income Tax, Dog License Tax, Excise Taxes, Federal Income Tax, Federal Unemployment Tax (FUTA), Fishing License Tax, Food License Tax, Fuel Permit Tax, Gasoline Tax, Gross Receipts Tax, Hunting License Tax, Inheritance Tax, Inventory Tax, IRS Interest and Penalties (tax on top of tax), Liquor Tax, Luxury Taxes, Marriage License Tax, Medicare Tax, Personal Property Tax, Real Estate Tax, Road Usage Tax, Recreational

Vehicle Tax, Sales Tax, School Tax, Service Charge Tax, Social Security Tax, State Income Tax, State Unemployment Tax (SUTA), Telephone Federal Excise Tax, Telephone Federal Universal Service Fee Tax, Telephone State and Local Taxes, Utility Taxes, Vehicle License Registration Tax, Vehicle Sales Tax, Watercraft Registration Tax, Well Permit Tax, Workers Compensation Tax.

Now consider this: almost none of these taxes existed a century ago. For those whose memories don't go back that far, our nation was the most prosperous in the world, we had a small national debt, the largest middle class on earth, and mom stayed home to raise the kids. Today we are burdened with a multitude of taxes while more are being added all the time. We are facing overwhelming personal and national debt, constant worries about our economic future, and, typically, both parents have to work just to keep their snorkel above water. Obviously, something is wrong.

At the heart of what is wrong is a change in the operational philosophy of government. We have changed from a system that emphasized individual responsibility to one that emphasizes collective responsibility. (This is another consequence of the dominion held by the Progressive "*Tellers*" mentioned in Chapter One.) Under a system that emphasizes individual responsibility the formula is: "I want it; I buy it." Under collective responsibility the formula is: "I want it; you buy it." We try to lay the burden of paying for everything on everyone. The problem is that not everyone makes enough money to pay for their fair share, so someone else has to pay more than their fair share – which simply isn't fair.

In a nutshell, the government is trying to do too much. This, however, is not the result of the government being profoundly compassionate, as some would have you believe. The driving force behind big government is much more sinister. It boils down to this: if we the people depend upon the government to provide all the critical needs of our lives (jobs, economic development, education, pensions, healthcare, loans, utilities, security, etc.), then guess who has all the power – and guess who doesn't. We the people become the serfs of the politicians and bureaucrats. They no longer work for us. We work for them. Furthermore, this oppressive machine which they have created to keep them in power needs lots of fuel; and that fuel is wealth. The problem is that government doesn't make wealth; the government takes wealth. From where? From those who create the wealth, which is all of you who work hard to produce valuable goods and services.

Taxation in modern America is no longer about paying for the necessary functions of government. If you doubt my claim consider this: government currently spends most of the money it gets on programs and activities that didn't even exist for more than the first half of our history. If these were necessary functions, then how did we survive? For the most part, modern taxation has become a scheme to divert our money into the hands of the politicians so they can use it to buy enough votes to stay in power. They promise poor people food, welfare, and healthcare. They promise big businesses tax exemptions and bailouts. They promise big unions closed shops and guaranteed benefits. They promise non-union workers minimum wages. They promise farmers subsidies. They promise students low-cost loans. They promise non-students training programs. They promise minorities preferential treatment. They promise the elderly a pension and healthcare. They promise the handicapped a ramp and a rail; and so on, and so on, and so on. Of course, all of these promises promise all of us higher and more taxes to pay for it all. In fact, we'd be better off if we just cut off everybody's bribes and went back to a simple system of individual responsibility (that is, "I want it, I buy it"); but that would take away the politicians' leverage, which, as we said, is the ability to spend your money to buy someone else's vote.

So, how do we stop the politicians from reaching more deeply into our pockets whenever their coffers of corruption run low? A simple four-part program will work very nicely.

1. *Limit each level of government to one or two sources of tax revenue.*

Governments may impose a reasonable charge for services rendered, like issuing a passport, driver's license, or library card. They also may charge penalties for violations of the law, like traffic tickets or late payments. Other than this, they must be restricted to only one or two sources of additional revenue through taxation. Revenue sources would include such things as income, sales, property, and excised goods. For example, the federal government could be limited to income tax and maybe one other. State governments could be limited to sales tax and maybe one other. County governments could be limited to property tax and maybe one other. Cities could be limited to excise taxes on utilities and maybe one other. If we don't do this, we will continue to see the insane proliferation of taxes as detailed at the beginning of this chapter.

2. *Limit the amount which may be taken from each source of tax revenue.*

Not only must we limit the number of sources which the government may tap, we also must limit the amount it can take from each source. If we do not do this, the tax rate will keep going up to feed the growth of the beast. For example, we could limit income tax to a flat 9%. Limit sales tax to 5%, and so forth.

These two measures will hem our political spend-thrifts within a sturdy straightjacket that can restrain their prodigal tendencies; but they still allow sufficient slack for the creative politico to wriggle around and cause more mischief. Two more measures must be added to cinch the restraints.

3. *Government may not go into debt.*

Even if we limit the number of things which the politicians may tax and put a cap on the amount which may be taken from each source, we will still be destined to watch helplessly as things spin out of control through deficit spending. Once the government uses up all the duly limited resources that have been granted to it, it may still slip its restraints by borrowing against future revenue. This is an especially attractive and insidious tactic. It provides more money now (as well as the ability to purchase more votes) while inflicting no immediate pain upon the taxpayer. To be sure, however, the pain will come. The future will be burdened not only with its own expenses, but with the expenses of the past as well – plus interest. It is just like getting a loan for a car or a house which otherwise would be beyond our ability to acquire. We feel a euphoric rush as we are suddenly endowed with money we didn't have and with the ability to acquire an asset we couldn't afford. All is well – until we have to come up with the extra money in the future to pay for past extravagances. If we don't deny the politicians the power to tap the economic wellsprings of tomorrow in order to finance their schemes of today, we will find ourselves living in a very parched and desolate future.

Make no mistake about it – deficit spending is merely stealth taxation. If we want to limit our taxes, we must not only monitor what the government is spending today, we also must keep a watchful eye on what we permit it to borrow from tomorrow. The surest way to accomplish this is to forbid the government from going into debt. Live within your means, and your means will always be enough to live on.

4. *Government must fully fund all that it mandates.*

There is still one more door which must be nailed shut before we can be reasonably confident of having confined the beast. We must require the government to fully fund all its mandates from its own financial resources.

As we have already mentioned, a common mode of operation for politicians is to seduce some segment of the voting population with valuable benefits while having someone else pay the bill. First, they used tax dollars to fund this vote-buying; but taxes got high, voters began to complain, responsible parties were sought out, and the hue and cry went out, "Heads on pikes!" Well, that got the politicians' attention because it was their heads that were going to be mounted on the pole. "Maybe", they thought, "we shouldn't keep raising taxes." This sentiment didn't flow from any compassion for the suffering taxpayers, but rather from the fear of being kicked out of power. Still, they knew that they had a good thing going in being able to buy votes with someone else's money. So, they got creative, and "deficit spending" became the flavor of the month. But, as we said, deficit spending is stealth taxation; and when the taxpayer began to feel the pinch from higher taxes and inflation, the old familiar chant, "Heads on pikes!" was heard again across the land. Did the politicians feel the need to lessen the misery of the tax-paying masses? Of course not. They felt the need to get creative again, and so they came up with still another ploy: unfunded mandates. Well, at least they were unfunded by the government, which the politicians hoped would divert attention off of them long enough to get re-elected a few more times before the citizenry got wise and again began to call for more heads on pikes.

Here's how it works in principle: Imagine that you want to impress your date (the vote you want to buy) with an expensive meal. You go to the finest restaurant in town and order the priciest thing on the menu (the mandate). You then direct the server to give the check to some poor, unsuspecting sap across the room. You got the girl, you got the meal, and someone else got the bill. That's how unfunded mandates work. Now let's look at a real example.

In 1990 Congress passed the Americans with Disabilities Act (ADA). The expressed purpose of this bill was to prevent discrimination based on disability and to make the American way of life more accessible to the handicapped – something only a moral monster could oppose. Lots of expensive changes would be required in order to comply with the requirements of the act, but very little of that expense would be paid by tax dollars. Well, then, where would the money come from? Businesses, of course. Uncounted billions of dollars have been spent retrofitting existing structures – which met construc- tion codes when they were first built – in order to install ramps at precisely the right gradient, rip out old doors and install new ones a few inches wider, and make sure the center of toilets were a minimum of eighteen inches from the wall – along with a myriad of other structural and nonstructural requirements. These mandates strangled – in some cases to death – thousands of businesses while creating a boon for ambulance-chasing (or in this case, wheelchair-chasing) attorneys, some of whom sent out handicapped individuals looking for any infractions so they could make a lucrative income by suing business owners for non-compliance. (I suppose it is a mere co-incidence that there are more lawyers in Congress than there are members from any other profession.)

This tactic was ingenious from the big-spenders' perspective, and once again we see malevolence and ignorance ally to form a masterful tag team. The politicians succeeded in buying themselves yet another constituency – the disabled – and what was even better, the taxpayers generally took no offense because they didn't see their taxes go up one whit as a result of the new law. (There were minor impositions on government funds in order to pay for the retrofitting of some government facilities – but nothing so significant that anyone really noticed.) Sadly, few taxpayers stopped to think that they also are consumers, and almost anything that causes the cost of business to go up will also cause an increase in the cost of the goods and services purchased from those businesses. So, while John and Jane Public were carefully guarding their right pocket, the politicians were skillfully picking the left one. If the taxpayer had clearly seen up front how much it would cost him to pay for these measures, he might have thought twice about how dear they were to him. Certainly, everyone wants to see handicapped people have access to the same amenities as everyone else – until he is handed a bill for an extra three or four hundred dollars a year to accomplish it. Mind you, I am not saying that these measures should not be taken. I am saying that we need to be honest about their true cost – especially with those who will be paying the bill.

*   *   *

This simple four-part program will go a very long way toward constraining our spendthrift politicians and bureaucrats and retaining the money that we taxpayers earned. However, there is another critical issue related to government expenditures which must be addressed: mega-emergencies. Such things as wars and natural disasters can impose significant, unexpected expenses on a society which may far outstrip the resources of a prudent budget. How can the government get the funding needed to address these needs?

We must build a contingency plan for emergencies into our program for financing government operations. This plan will allow for the raising of additional revenue to address the crisis, but it must include the following measures in order to prevent abuse.

1. The additional revenue must come from one of the sources already approved for taxation. No new sources will be allowed. Creating new and unfamiliar sources will be more difficult

to monitor and control and, accordingly, more prone to abuse.

2. The additional emergency revenues will be obtained by increasing the taxation cap. This increase will be specifically defined and not open-ended (for example, raising the individual income tax from nine to eleven percent, or sales tax from five to seven percent).

3. The additional revenue may only be spent on the purpose for which they were designated, like disaster relief or wartime expenditures.

4. Permission to collect this surcharge will have a "Sunset Clause"; in other words, it expires after a certain, specified period of time, like two or three years. At that time the rate of taxation reverts to the previous level unless extended through the procedure described in Part 5 below.

5. The above terms must be submitted in a plebi-scite (a yes or no vote) to all eligible voters and approved by a super-majority of sixty-five percent. The requirement for a super-majority is essential. Without it politicians can pursue new ambitions anytime they happen to muster the support of a mere majority of the people. This requirement also insures that a substantial portion of the voters agree about the worthiness of these expenditures.

Back in Chapter Six we described the "Holy Trinity" of rights: life, property, and liberty. Included among an individual's legitimate property rights are his honest earnings. It is the responsibility of government to protect this right – not to abuse it. Some taxation is necessary, but it must be conducted in a manner consistent with the desires of those who provide the revenue, and it must be used to provide some definite benefit to the taxpayer. This is not what is happening at present. As was mentioned above, taxation in modern America is no longer about paying for the essential functions of government. Taxation in modern America has become a scheme to divert our money into the hands of the politicians so they can use it to buy enough votes to stay in power. This is an egregious violation of the public trust; it is a betrayal of the most sacred responsibility of government; it is grounds for we the people "to alter or to abolish" the offending government.

CHAPTER NINE

HE WHO PAYS THE NICKEL CALLS THE TUNE; REDEFINING VOTER "RIGHTS"

The Declaration of Independence makes it very clear that the most fundamental responsibility of government is to "secure these rights" that were "endowed" by the "Creator." Which rights? Well, "among these are Life, Liberty ... the pursuit of Happiness", and "to alter or abolish" any government that "becomes destructive of these ends...." Okay, but what are the rights which may be included "among" – or in addition to – those specifically mentioned? The Declaration is strangely silent. What is more, so is the Constitution – so silent that many Americans back in 1787 felt that they could not support this new plan of government unless these rights were specifically delineated. And so, a deal was struck. The supporters of the proposed Constitution agreed to add several amendments spelling out these rights if the skeptics would agree to endorse the document. Enough skeptics went along with this compromise that it was possible to win ratification. The Constitution's supporters kept their promise. They drafted and approved a Bill of Rights before the end of the first legislative session of the First Congress. This Bill of Rights comprises the first ten amendments to the Constitution. It was passed September 25, 1789, and ratified December 15, 1791.

So, what were the rights that were included "among these" other ones? Well, there were freedom of religion, speech, press, assembly, petition, and to keep and bear arms. We also were free from quartering troops, unreasonable searches and seizures, and other abuses of police and prosecutorial power including double jeopardy and being forced to testify against oneself. Our lives, liberty, and property could not be taken without due process. Private property could not be seized for public use without fair compensation. We had the right to a speedy trial decided by a jury of our peers after being informed of the charges against us while being confronted by our accusers. Other rights involving civil trials were described. No excessive bail nor cruel and unusual punishment could be meted out. It also was stated that a right was not necessarily denied to the people just because it wasn't mentioned in any of these amendments. And then we wrapped the whole thing up by noting that unless a power was specifically awarded to the federal government or denied to the states, that power could be claimed by the states or the people.

Notice anything missing? What about voting? Does that mean that we the people do not have the right to vote? Not necessarily. However, since the responsibility of defining voters' rights is not a power "delegated to the United States [federal government] by the Constitution, nor prohibited by it to the states," it is "reserved to the states respectively, or to the people" – as stated in the Tenth Amendment. In other words, voting rights are to be defined by the states or smaller jurisdictions. This may seem strange to the modern ear, but it was entirely consistent with conventional practice at the time the Constitution was written and implemented.

Prior to the ratification of the Fourteenth Amendment (July 9, 1868), the definition and rights of citizenship were determined largely at the local or state level. The word "citizen" derives from the Old French word, "citeien" which means "city dweller." We might think of a "citizen" as a "**cit**y den**izen**." The rights and privileges of citizenship varied geographically and were determined by the city or region in which one resided. Included among these rights and privileges were voting and property ownership. What's more, citizenship was not automatic. It was not awarded to someone simply because he could maintain a body temperature in the vicinity of 98.6 degrees. The citizen was expected to be a contributing member of the society. "Contributing member" was defined differently in different locals, but defining criteria could include such things as education, community service, property ownership, paying taxes, and in some cases, the good fortune of noble birth. With the exception of "noble birth," this is the conception of citizenship that would have been held by our Founders. Their notion of citizenship would likely be consistent with the standards published by Emerich de Vattel in his *Law of Nations*. Within the nineteenth volume of that work, it says, "The citizens are the members of the civil society; bound to this society by certain duties, and subject to its authority, they equally participate in its advantages." In other words, the rights of citizenship would be equally enjoyed **once a person qualified for them** by performing certain duties and obeying the law. Once earned, citizenship could be revoked if a person failed to perform necessary duties or violated certain laws.

It was possible for a foreigner to become a citizen (naturalized citizen), but the first rank of citizenship was the "natural born citizen." According to de Vattel, a natural born citizen was not merely someone who was born in the city, region, or nation; but one who was born "of a father who is a citizen; for, if he is born there of a foreigner, it will be only the place of his birth, and not his country." Thus, to qualify as a natural born citizen, one had to be born in the territory of a father who is a citizen of that territory. Why? Loyalty. A citizen owes his utmost secular allegiance to his homeland. Merely being born in a specific territory was not sufficient to secure this loyalty. In short, no citizen-father, no natural born citizen status.

This all started to change with the Fourteenth Amendment. The Emancipation Proclamation (an executive order issued January 1, 1863) officially established the goals of ending slavery throughout the United States and granting citizenship to those who had been slaves. The Union victory in the Civil War made these objectives possible, and the Thirteenth Amendment sealed the deal. Still, many feared that the rights and privileges of full citizenship would continue to be denied to former slaves unless further action was taken. Hence, the Fourteenth. Among other things, this amendment declared that everyone born in the United States or naturalized therein and who is subject to its jurisdiction is a United States citizen. Citizenship was no longer determined at the local or state level. It had become a national right. Furthermore, the requirement of being a "contributing member" was eliminated. Citizenship had become an unearned gift granted to all who were born or naturalized here and subject to the jurisdiction of the United States. This amendment expanded citizenship much like the bomb expanded Hiroshima – it was huge and devastating. On the other hand, its impact on voting privileges – though significant – was not quite so comprehensive.

A careful reading of Section 2 of the Fourteenth Amendment reveals that voting rights were not specifically granted to all citizens. However, it does state that if voting is denied to any male who is at least twenty-one years old, the "basis of representation" for that state "shall be reduced in the proportion which the number of such male citizens shall bear to the whole number of male citizens twenty-one years of age in such State." In other words, if a state denies citizens their voting privileges, it's going to cost that state some power in the Congress and the Electoral College. Although the Fourteenth's expansion of voting privileges was not as comprehensive as its expansion of citizenship, its impact was considerable. More was to come.

The Fifteenth Amendment stated that, "The right of citizens of the United States to vote shall not be denied or abridged by the United States or by any state on account of race, color, or previous condition of servitude." The Nineteenth Amendment extended the right to vote to women. The Twenty-fourth Amendment said that voting rights could not be denied or abridged for "failure to pay any poll tax or other tax." Then the Twenty-sixth Amendment dropped the minimum age requirement to eighteen.

The cumulative effect of all this was to make voting an unearned, free gift extended to everyone born or naturalized here and subject to our national jurisdiction once he or she became eighteen years of age. So, what possibly could be wrong with this? Well, for starters, we just institutionalized one of the greatest nightmares of the Founders. For all practical purposes, we just turned our Republic into a Democracy. The countdown to disaster had begun.

The ancients and not-so-ancients had been very wise to tie citizenship to being a "contributing member" of the society. Those who contribute to the spiritual and material best interests of a society often have a very different perspective and set of values from those who do not contribute. The contributors' perspective, values, and resultant actions are more likely to strengthen and safeguard a nation than those of non-contributors. There is no attempt to be pollyannaish here. Contributors are often selfish – sometimes viciously so – but they are selfish in ways that usually enrich others and strengthen the nation as well as themselves. This is not the case with non-contributors. Non-contributors have a different set of interests, and catering to those interests works to weaken and impoverish the nation. Does this mean that their interests should be ignored? Certainly not – especially in the case of those who are involuntarily non-contributors – like the infirm. They deserve our compassion and support on a freewill basis. However, those who choose to live the life of a non-contributor deserve nothing more than a pointed lesson on self-sufficiency – and they certainly do not deserve to vote. Extending suffrage privileges to the non-contributors only allows them to vote themselves into the pockets of the contributors which, in turn, undermines the long-term security of the entire nation. This is the poison pill of democracy. It is why they always fail. Sooner or later the non-contributors – and those who hope to join their ranks – learn that they can tax the contributors in order to finance their lazy lifestyle. Eventually, there is not enough water to support all the sponges, and the whole system dries up. This is why the Founders loathed democracy. This is why the Fourteenth, Fifteenth, Nineteenth, Twenty-fourth, and Twenty-sixth Amendments were ill-written. This is why the countdown to disaster has begun.

Please note: I did not say these amendments were ill-advised. I said they were ill-written. I do not oppose opening voting to members of these groups. What I do oppose is blanket statements that **all** members of any race or **all** members of either sex or **all** people of a certain age should be granted the privilege, because not all of them are contributing members – and this **should** be a blanket requirement.

If we are to regain the blessings which flowed from the wisdom of the Founders, then we must reestablish a system which honors and implements their wisdom. The focus of this chapter is citizenship and its attendant voting privileges, so let us now turn our attention to the issue of defining citizenship and determining who gets to vote. Should citizenship remain an unearned, free gift, or should someone actually have to qualify for receiving the benefits of a nation and for enjoying the privilege of determining its course?

A person has to prove that he is reasonably competent and familiar with legal procedures in order to get a driver's license. One has to prove that he is reasonably competent and familiar with basic information to get a diploma. One has to prove that he is reasonably competent and familiar with basic vocational skills to get a job. So, why shouldn't one have to prove that he is reasonably competent and familiar with relevant social issues before he is entrusted with the responsibility and power to help shape local, state, and national policy? The idea is simple: you don't give someone a job that he doesn't deserve and can't handle.

The same idea applies to the job of citizenship and voting. Accordingly, we must reestablish reasonable criteria that must be met before citizenship and voting privileges are granted. What are these criteria?

*   *   *

Natural Born versus Naturalized. The Constitution distinguishes between these two categories of citizens, and so should we. We also should follow de Vattel's lead in defining a "natural born citizen" as someone who was born in the country and whose father is a citizen of this country. Additionally, we need to include in this category those who are born outside the country if their father is a citizen and the birth takes place during a temporary leave of absence from the country – like military or diplomatic service, business trip, vacation, or other temporary absence. Keep in mind, however, that mere birth and parentage are not sufficient to qualify for citizenship. The above criteria will be necessary to qualify for "natural born" status once the other requirements are met. A "naturalized citizen" shall be any other person who was not born in the country and/or who does not have a citizen father but who meets the other criteria for citizenship.

Education. A person cannot do a job without a sufficiency of knowledge in areas relevant to performing that job. Mere volume of knowledge is not good enough. It must be relevant knowledge. Cardiologists are very

123

well-educated, but we don't let them perform brain surgery. Similarly, citizenship and voting privileges must be tied to a sufficiency of relevant knowledge. In this case that knowledge must be in such areas as language skills and literature, history, economics, morals, mathematics, science, politics and government, human behavior, reasoning, etc. We need to restructure our school system in order to provide students with a sufficiency of knowledge in these areas so that they may meet the educational requirements for citizenship by the time they complete high school. Obviously, I am talking about an educational system that does a much better and different job than our current failure. **Once this restructuring of our school system is accomplished**, the educational requirement for citizenship and voting privileges can be considered satisfied by receiving a high school diploma or its equivalent.

Contributing Member. A battle cry of the first American Revolution was "No taxation without representation!" The argument was a simple one. If our money is going to be used to finance the government, then we who provide this money should have a say in how much money is taken and where it is spent. In short, the interests of the people paying the bill need to be represented. That sounds eminently fair. He who provides the nickel gets to call the tune. But every coin has two sides, and the same is true for most coined phrases – like "No taxation without representation." If it is fair to argue that someone should not be taxed unless he is represented, is it not also fair to argue that someone should not be represented unless he is taxed? This brings us to the larger issue of being a "contributing member" of a society in order to qualify for citizenship and voting privileges.

Those who have no "skin in the game" are not likely to be especially concerned about which way the game goes. We simply **cannot** allow those who make little or no contribution to the society to have the power to decide its course. At best they will likely be poor judges of what it takes to maintain a successful society. At worst, they are likely to have personal interests contrary to those who do contribute to the society. The non-contributors can be expected to use the power of citizenship and their franchise to vote their way into the contributors' pockets – which, as we said earlier, is how democracies begin their death spiral.

If we **cannot** allow those who make little or no contribution to the society to have the power to decide its course, then we **must** establish criteria for determining who is a "contributing member." For one thing, a contributing member must be financially self-sufficient. By definition, if one is not financially self-sufficient then one is not contributing economically. These non-contributors are the very people whom the Founders feared, for they are the assassins of democracies. These are the very people who will use their franchise to seize the wealth created by the contributors and destroy their incentive to be productive.

In Chapter Ten of *Solutions: Guidebook for Rebuilding America the Great*, I argued that, "National service is a national obligation and a personal responsibility owed by one and by all. Accordingly, the United States should adopt a system of national service by all its citizens." I will not repeat all the reasons for this policy here other than to quote the summary remark, "We all share an obligation to support and defend our nation, and we all should be proud to do so." It therefore follows that another requirement of citizenship must be to have completed some form of national service. This does not have to be military in nature, but it must fall in the realm of some designated service that is personally sacrificial and socially beneficial. (See Chapter Ten of *Solutions* for specifics.) There is a big difference between Americans and people who simply live in America. The type of national service envisioned in *Solutions* will contribute significantly to the development of Americans; and this is the kind of identity and loyalty that is necessary to make good citizens.

Contributing members must also be law-abiding. Classic definitions of "citizenship", like de Vattel's, refer to being "subject to its [the region's or nation's] authority." This not only means that a person lives under the authority of the law of the land but also that he adheres to it. Laws are written to modify behavior in such ways as to encourage the accomplishment of a society's goals. Those who violate the law (generally speaking, but not in every case – like righteous rebels, for example, Washington, Adams, Jefferson, Franklin, Hancock, Henry, etc.) work at cross-purposes to a society's goals and, by definition, are not contributing to that society. Accordingly, we must establish standards of legal behavior in order to achieve and maintain citizenship and voting privileges. At a minimum, those convicted of a felony ought to be disqualified from citizenship – at least for a specified period of time. Repeat offenders and those who commit especially serious crimes can be disqualified for life.

In addition to being law-abiding, a person also must be moral to qualify for citizenship. There is an intimate relationship between the fields of law and morals. Although there are those who argue that we should not legislate morals, this is an absurd notion. Virtually all legislation flows from some moral precept and – superficially at least – works to accomplish some moral objective. So, how does this relate to citizenship?

Immoral people should be disqualified from citizenship and voting privileges. That proposition alone will be difficult for some (especially the immoral) to swallow. Hang on. It's going to get worse. As is argued elsewhere in this book, morality is not manmade. It is the province of God. Accordingly, one cannot be moral if one is unGodly. At a minimum, this disqualifies atheists from citizenship.

"WHOA! Stop the presses!", the reader may be saying. "You said that the most sacred responsibility of governments was to protect rights, and the First Amendment guarantees the right to believe whatever you want about God!"

Dear reader, if you believe this, you have been duped. (And you thought I was being harsh when I referred to our school system as a "failure" a few paragraphs ago.) The First Amendment guarantees no such thing. Read it. The First Amendment states that Congress may not establish a state church nor prohibit anyone from practicing his religion. Since most definitions of "religion" speak of a belief in some supernatural power – which atheists deny – atheism is not a religion and therefore not protected. The Constitution is primarily concerned about the freedom **of** religion, not a freedom **from** religion – another area in which you undoubtedly have been mislead by our schools – and others.

But, let me help you argue your case. In Article Six of the Constitution it states that, "no religious test shall ever be required as a qualification to any office or public trust under the United States." This is the passage that would seem to counter my argument that some measure of morality must be a criterion for citizenship and voting privileges; and that atheists, in particular, should be disqualified. Don't start celebrating just yet. The passage immediately before the one just quoted states that, "The Senators and Representatives before mentioned, and the members of the several state legislatures, and all executive and judicial officers, both of the United States and of the several states, shall be bound by oath or affirmation, to support this Constitution...." What the Constitution giveth, the Constitution taketh away. The Founders, including the drafters of the Constitution, understood the word, "oath" to be a promise to God. Atheists cannot take an oath because they do not believe in God. No God, no promise. No promise, no oath. No oath, no office-holding. So, if you insist that atheists be allowed to be citizens, then "citizenship" must be defined in a way that it does not include the privilege to hold or run for office, since atheists cannot do so by virtue of their inability to take an oath. Either your way or mine, atheists will be excluded from holding office, so why complicate the definition of "citizenship" further just to accommodate atheists?

Although this notion regarding atheists may sound strange to us today, it is not at all contrary to common practice throughout most of our history. Up until the 1950s it was commonplace to exclude atheists from serving on juries, testifying in court, and holding public office. Why? Because they could not take an oath. Without a belief in God, their word could not be trusted. In effect, the Founders were willing to acknowledge one's free will to reject the existence of God, but they were not willing to trust them, and neither should we. We may have to tolerate them, but we don't have to allow them to help shape our policies and future.

A few paragraphs ago I stated that, "Immoral people should be disqualified from citizenship and voting privileges." Other than atheism, what criteria for immorality should be used to disqualify from citizenship? Personally, I am rather fond of Biblical standards; but I would recommend that we work toward this and not start there. If we did, we might not have enough candidates to staff the

Congress, much less vote for them. I would be content, initially, to begin with the previously mentioned standard of law-abiding behavior and then work to expand the scope of the law to include more morally-based offenses.

Morality is an indispensable element of good citizenship. I would like to conclude this section on morality by reminding you of the words of Charles Carroll. Unfortunately, I cannot "remind" the reader of something he has never heard; and considering the abject failure of our school system, you are probably completely unfamiliar with what was written by this signer of the Declaration of Independence – so let me "introduce" you to his profound wisdom. "[W]ithout morals a republic cannot subsist any length of time; they therefore who are decrying the Christian religion, whose morality is so sublime and pure ... are undermining the solid foundation of morals, the best security for the duration of free governments."

Age. Age would no longer be a specific requirement for citizenship. By the time an individual fulfilled all the other requirements, he could reasonably be expected to be minimally qualified for citizenship regardless of his age.

Oath. Upon meeting the minimum requirements for citizenship specified, the candidate for citizenship and voting privileges must consummate the process by taking an oath which minimally obligates the candidate to preserve, protect, and defend the Constitution of the

United States. Here, again, atheists would be disqualified for they cannot take an oath.

*   *   *

The above standards specify what should be the minimum requirements for earning citizenship and voting privileges. Citizenship and voting privileges may also be lost and reinstated. Grounds for losing citizenship and voting privileges should be the obverse of the standards for achieving citizenship. If one ceases to be self-sufficient for a specified period of time, or is convicted of committing a felony or some specified moral turpitude, or becomes an atheist, then one's citizenship and voting privileges may be revoked. Furthermore, remember that the whole justification for these criteria is to insure that we grant citizenship to people who are competent for the task. Accordingly, those who are or have become mentally incompetent may be disqualified. And, of course, citizenship and voting privileges may be reinstated when the disqualifying circumstance is remediated – unless a permanent revocation is justified by somethings such as committing an especially heinous crime.

*   *   *

The powers of citizenship and of voting are simply too critical to the survival and success of a nation to be granted indiscriminately as an unearned, free gift. You would not ride in a bus driven by someone who was not a competent driver. You would not agree to a serious operation to be performed by someone who was not a competent surgeon. You would not hire someone who was not a competent contractor to build your house. So, why should we allow incompetents to decide the course of a nation?

These recommendations will be opposed by the incompetent and by the deceitful politicians who count on their votes. The corrupt and unscrupulous politicians will tell you that, "We need to keep moving forward, but Hebron's proposals will move us backward!" Actually, backward is a pretty good direction if you are headed for a cliff. And as for the incompetents who will be disqualified? My advice is simple: stop being incompetent and get qualified. With the exception of serious felons and the permanently infirm and mentally incompetent, there are virtually no comprehensive and insurmountable disqualifiers mentioned above. If you're not well-educated, get an education. If you're not self-sufficient, get a job. If you're a criminal, stop. If you're an atheist, look around. God was messy. He left His fingerprints everywhere. Open your eyes and discover the truth.

The blessings of citizenship are too precious to be enjoyed by those who don't deserve them. The power of citizenship is too great to be wielded by those who haven't earned it. We need to return to those values which served us so well in the past. Remember, when you start on a mountaintop, don't move. The only way to go is down.

CHAPTER TEN

MONEY IS POWER. WHO CONTROLS YOURS; PAYROLL AND COMPENSATION REFORM

Money is power. Control the way a worker is paid, and you control the worker. Control the worker, and you control the nation. The mechanics of the political machine have long understood this. They also have understood that Americans do not submit easily to harness and whip. We have proved to be a rebellious lot and fiercely defensive of our liberties. This does not mean that Americans cannot be broken and enslaved. It just means that the would-be masters have to go about their task creatively so it doesn't look like they are doing what they are doing. Or should I say, "that it didn't look like they have done what they have done." The truth is that the American worker has already been harnessed – that he already is enslaved.

Do you doubt this? Then ask yourself a simple question. "Who owns your life?" There are many ways to approach this question, so there also are many possible answers. For now, however, let us consider the question from a historical and economic perspective. From this point of view, the issue of who owns – or controls – your life is decided by the answer to this question: "Who controls the wealth that you create?" Let us briefly consider this.

First, a quick review from Econ 101. "Wealth" does not consist of pieces of paper with the pictures of presidents or other dignitaries on them. Nor does it consist of shiny, thin discs of pretty metal. Wealth consists of goods (things) and services (actions and advice) that people value enough that they are willing to trade other goods and services in order to acquire them. Strictly speaking, "money" is not wealth. "Money" is simply a means of measuring and exchanging wealth. (Oh the problems we would avoid if more people understood this!) For the sake of simplicity, however, I will use money as a representation of wealth in the following example.

Suppose that you were a worker who "grossed" $1,000 per pay period – be it a week, two weeks, month, whatever. Your "net" or "take-home" pay would be $800-ish. Sadly, it is important that I add the "ish." Our current payroll system is so complicated and convoluted that I cannot give a more precise accounting of net pay than this in the given example. There simply are too many variables, but this amount is a reasonable approximation.

"Well", you may be thinking, "controlling 80% of my income isn't too bad. I guess I do own my life." Poor schmuck, that's exactly what the mechanics want you to think. In fact, there is much more to the matter than this. The typical employer spends far more on the typical employee than the gross. There are also employer contributions to such things as Social Security and Medicare and state unemployment tax and federal unemployment tax and workers' compensation and disability. These alone are likely to add another twelve to fifteen percent to the cost of the employee to the employer – and maybe much more. When you consider that over and above this amount many employers make still more contributions to such things as the employee's healthcare and pensions and life insurance, this amount jumps even higher. It is not unusual for an employer to spend an additional twenty-five to thirty percent over and above the gross on his employees. So, that $1,000 gross turns into a $1,300 "super-gross." This is what the employer is really spending on this employee, even though the employee only gets to take home $800–ish. He's not really controlling 80% of his earnings. It's more like 61.5%. Do you still think it's such a good deal? Well, it gets worse.

By the time this "typical" employee gets his payroll check in his hot little hands, he has already lost control of almost forty cents of every dollar he earned. Once he deposits the check and starts to spend it, the government gives him ample opportunities to lose even more control. If his state has sales tax, he gets to lose several more percentage points of ownership. Property tax will siphon off still more. And then come all the excise taxes on phone, utilities, and other items. Ever use gasoline? There goes still more money into the state and federal coffers. (By the way, the federal government makes several times more money on a gallon of gas than the oil companies. And the oil companies are called "greedy!" At least they worked for their income. All the government did was pass a law.) Do you smoke or drink or occasionally use a motel? There goes more control over your money. By the time you add up all these government taxes and fees, you've lost control of more than half of your income. But we're just warming up. Or, should I say, "worming" up.

The government has several other stealthy ways of taking control of your money for their purposes. Every year you lose a measure of purchasing power to inflation. The common misperception is that costs go up because of greedy businesses that raise prices or because of greedy unions that raise wages. There is some negligible increase in inflation because of this, but the main thrust for the increase in prices – and the erosion of your purchasing power – comes from the monetary policy carried out by an unholy alliance between the federal government and the Federal Reserve System – which is controlled by a banking cartel and is not part of the federal government, as many believe.

But wait, there's more – if I may quote your favorite infomercial. Government subsidies and bailouts cost us wealth-creaters additional billions every year – and our control over our income becomes smaller and smaller.

But wait, there's – oh, yeah, I already said that. But there is more! Certain government policies favor particular agendas – and particular voters – at our considerable expense, even though this never shows up on our tax bills. Consider gasoline. We have enough proven petroleum reserves in the United States to satisfy our fossil fuel needs for roughly one century without relying on a single drop from foreign sources. So, why have we created an artificial shortage which drives up prices and increases our dependence upon foreign suppliers – many of whom don't like us very well? You can bet somebody is winning from this action, but it ain't us. (Apologies to all you English teachers – assuming you caught that.) If we merely announced that we were going to open every spigot we've got – from ANWR (Arctic National Wildlife Refuge) to the Gulf of Mexico, and from sea to shining sea – we'd see gasoline prices drop significantly in weeks. If we were to follow up and pursue this goal, we'd see gas prices cut perhaps in half within two to three years. Here again, the government is controlling your money for their purposes.

Now, add up all these factors and you will find that many Americans only control somewhere between 30% to 40% of the money their employer spends on them. There is a word that historians have used to describe workers who only get to enjoy a small percentage of the wealth they create. Slave. I surely hope that we are still the home of the brave, because we are most definitely no longer the land of the free; and we need to do something about it. Government has stealthily seized control of our lives by taking control of our wealth – which was pretty much the complaint of the colonists in 1775. We all know where that led. So, what are we going to do about it?

First, let us look at how the current twisted system of payroll and compensation came about. Then we will examine an amazingly simple reform proposal that can:

> * Increase take-home pay by upwards of 40% without increasing payroll costs
> * Save our pensions
> * Return control of his destiny to the American worker
> * Reduce the cost and complexity of bookkeeping for thousands of businesses
> * Expand private industry and make your state attractive to new business
> * Create jobs
> * Encourage a responsible, productive citizenry
> * Cut the oppressive cost and influence of government at all levels

History. Workers have always been compensated for their labors. Initially their payment was "in kind." A helper might work for a farmer in exchange for a sack of grain that could be ground into flour to feed his family. Another worker might help a cobbler in exchange for a pair of shoes. Barter, however, was not very efficient, so we developed money to measure and exchange wealth.

Eventually, virtually all payment for labor in advanced economies was in the form of money. But then, several decades ago, something strange began to happen. Under the guise of wrenching additional concessions from the employer, and to get around certain labor laws, many workers began to receive benefits instead of money as part of their compensation package – payments "in kind" in addition to cash. These benefits included such things as pensions, healthcare, life insurance, unemployment insurance, workers' compensation insurance, disability pay, etc. To the worker it seemed like a good thing, but it was done in a bad way. Although these were important benefits for the worker, the worker was not in charge of them – he had no control. Since the benefit was provided by the employer or the union or the government, it was the employer or the union or the government that controlled the benefit. If the worker lost or changed his job, he could lose the benefit. If the employer or union or government were incompetent or dishonest, the worker could lose the benefit. If the future didn't pan out like the employer or the union or the government had promised, the worker could lose the benefit – or, at least, a substantial part of it. In fact, this is exactly what has happened to millions of workers across the country, and it is likely to happen to millions more. It is a calamity of epic proportions. Sadly, it was all so unnecessary. Happily, it is easy to fix.

Solution. So, how do we easily fix a problem that seems so massive and intractable? **Simply give every**

employee – public and private – 100% of the money that is spent on him. That would include his wages or salary plus all that is paid by the employer for various benefits – including those benefits currently entrusted to various government agencies. Let the employee, himself, decide for himself what to do with his own money. He earned it. Why shouldn't he have the freedom to control what happens to it? The worker could choose an optimal mix of spending, savings, and investment in various benefits – like pensions, healthcare, life insurance, unemployment insurance, workers' compensation, etc. Furthermore, the employee could move or change jobs without losing benefits because the benefits would be tied to the worker, not the work, nor the union, nor the government, as is presently the case. The employee would have the opportunity to shop around for less costly and more lucrative benefits than are currently provided. He would achieve a greater degree of personal liberty and control over key areas of his life. The oppressive power of the employer, the unions, and – especially – the government would be undermined and lessened. Payroll procedures for employers – public and private – would be simplified and made far less time-consuming and costly. Furthermore, trillions of dollars would be freed up for investment in private companies, thereby fueling the economy and creating jobs.

Admittedly, not all of this could be achieved immediately. Legislative action would be required to free the current payroll and tax systems from the arcane and twisted procedures which currently exist. Despite this, some significant reforms could be initiated without further delay. Most significantly, this could take place in the area of employee pensions. How? Simply take all the funds which are being contributed to the employee's pension plan and pay them directly to the employee who could invest them as he sees fit.

At this point I want to focus a little extra attention on the matter of pensions. The simple plan that has been proposed covers all aspects of a worker's payroll and compensation. Pensions, however, have become a major issue in recent years and will only get bigger. We can't seem to go very long before we are confronted with another news article about the failing Social Security system or another bankrupt public pension fund. Add to this the fact that the first of the Baby Boomers just hit retirement age, with tens of millions more in line behind them, and it becomes pretty obvious that if we don't take care of our pension plans, our pension plans will not be able to take care of us.

The plan described above would work well for those currently in the labor force. Simply take all the funds which are being contributed to the employee's pension plan and pay them directly to the employee who can invest them as he sees fit. But what about those who already have a substantial investment in a pension plan? If they are happy with it, especially if it is fully funded, they can simply keep it. They also have the option to cash it out – that is, pull out whatever they have invested in the plan. Many pension plans, however – especially those offered by various government agencies – face significant unfunded future liabilities. The enrollees in these plans face the likely prospect of receiving far less than they were promised. How do we deal with them? We cash out their holdings following this simple formula. We calculate how many dollars have been contributed to the plan on an employee's behalf. Each dollar invested represents one share. Count the total number of shares that exist among all those who have participated in the plan. Divide this number into the total real value of the pension fund. That determines how much each share is worth. Cash out the pension fund and distribute the proceeds to the enrollees (current and future retirees who have contributed to the fund) according to the number of shares they have. Allow them to reinvest this payout as they see fit to secure their best interests. If they roll over all or any part of this amount into another pension fund, there will be no tax consequence on this investment.

Under this reform plan, pensions and other benefits derive funding solely from compensation paid to the employee for work done by the employee. The amount of dollars available to finance pension funds will be the same under this new plan as before its implementation. The main thing that will change is that the worker will once again have control over his earnings. Well, this is true for **honest** pension plans. However, there are some not-so-honest plans that have been crafted by politicians to buy the votes of various government employees.

Many of these government plans are supplemented covertly by taxpayer contributions. This is a devious practice employed by unscrupulous politicians to buy the votes of public sector employees while burdening the citizenry they are supposed to be representing by forcing them, covertly, to pay for benefits which the citizens themselves do not get. This is a profoundly unjust practice and should be eliminated on its own demerits.

It is also true that many public employee pension funds have been misrepresented to workers, badly managed, or actually raided by government officials in order to alleviate their own fiscal difficulties. This has sometimes resulted in pension plans being significantly underfunded. Frankly, there is little chance of rescuing them without crushing new taxes or drastically reducing promised pay-outs in the future. In short, many public employee pensions are likely to collapse in the near future anyway. Why not be honest about the situation, cash out these pension funds, and return control to the worker while there is still time to avoid a catastrophe?

It is an unpleasant fact that implementing this plan – as it has been described thus far – will result in many public sector employees receiving substantially less than they were promised by the deceitful politicians who engineered their retirement plans. We could chastise these employees for not being wary of politicians bearing gifts that sounded too good to be true and simply let them suffer the consequences of their own foolishness. We could – but they, at least, have worked for a living; so maybe we, at least, owe them the responsibility to be as creative in rescuing them as the politicians were in fleecing them. Are there any reasonable and affordable options for saving the public employee's retirement? Yes.

First of all, let's be honest and admit that this nasty situation (namely, the underfunding of public pensions) is not the result of implementing this plan. The need to implement this plan is very much the result of this nasty situation. The plan was formulated, in part, to deal with the reality of an unsustainable pension system. It seeks to provide a managed transition from a dishonest, ineffectual, and nearly bankrupt system to one that is honest, effective, and funded. The failure to adopt such a managed transition will result in a devastating collapse that will shake and possibly shatter the economic foundation of our nation. Implementing the plan is our best and most responsible option. Still, there will be pain – especially for those who already are retired and those who soon will be. What can be done for them?

One way to help the worst victims of the mismanaged system mentioned above is through dedicated charities. Such charities would exist solely for the purpose of contributing to the retirement of the members of specific groups – like government clerks, postal workers, police, fire, nurses, teachers, etc. Such a plan follows an old American tradition of providing voluntary assistance to those in need. Its management would be outside of government control. This is essential. Remember, it was government mismanagement which caused the problem in the first place. It does not seem especially prudent to give the culprits a second chance to create mischief and spread misery.

A second, though far less advisable, option would be to finance a supplemental retirement fund through a locally implemented tax surcharge – like adding a quarter or half percent to existing sales tax rates for a specified period of time. The three most glaring difficulties with this idea are: (1) It would require a considerable degree of government involvement. In effect, we would turn to the problem-causer to be the problem-solver. Not wise. (2) It would be involuntarily imposed upon a significant number of people. Not American. (3) Excessive taxation already is draining too much fuel from the economic engines of our nation. Syphoning off even more fuel could cause those engines to shut down completely. Not sustainable.

There is a third alternative, however, which could fully fund our public pensions without costing the taxpayers an additional penny and without delaying retirements, reducing benefits, or increasing worker contributions. The money required to fully fund these pensions is already in the system – it simply is being misallocated. Across the land and at every level of government, unconscionable amounts of tax dollars are being allocated to nurture and perpetuate the profligate lifestyles of unproductive people. Still more is spent to aid and abet those who are in the country illegally. Simply divert some of this money into the underfunded pensions of those public employees who already are retired or who soon will be (say, within about 15 years) and you solve several problems simultaneously. Our firefighters, police officers, nurses, clerks, mail carriers, teachers, etc., will receive the compensation they were promised. Our able-bodied unproductives will learn to live responsibly and will soon become contributing members of the society. We will stop the morally and legally unsupportable practice of using taxpayer's money to subsidize lawbreakers who are in the country illegally while simultaneously reducing the incentive for others to follow their example.

By the way, this same model can be used to protect current and upcoming recipients of Social Security. Many politicians ask, "What can be done to save Social Security?" That is the wrong question. The right question is, "What can be done to save our seniors?" Social Security has been doomed since 1935 when Franklin Delano Roosevelt signed it into existence. It was based on faulty principles which have only gotten worse. It is a dead horse, and if you bet on it you lose. We shouldn't waste another second trying to save Social Security. It is a concrete life vest – it's going down. However, we can rescue pensioners – current and future – by following the plan described above. First, pay workers the money they earned and let them build their own pension funds – one that neither the boss, the union, nor the government can manipulate. Second, regarding those who already are retired or who soon will be, cash out the trust fund (if there really is one) and distribute it according to the formula presented above. Then supplement the shortfall from the hundreds of billions of dollars the federal government is currently spending on the unproductive and those in the country illegally. By doing this, we will immediately reduce the federal deficit (because we are spending far more on the unproductive and illegal immigrants than we do on our pensioners), see the amount of payout to pensions amortize in future years as the number of pensioners gradually drops to zero, and eliminate trillions of dollars of future unfunded liabilities – to name just a few benefits.

Dishonesty, bad management, and inattention by the electorate have conspired to create an unsustainable and dangerous situation. There is no painless way out; but there is an option that will help us avoid the most devastating consequences of the pension predicament. Take it or die. And in the future, never let anyone else – especially politicians and bureaucrats – take control over those areas of your life which are most critical to you.

Now back to the plan in general.

Concerns. Such a plan would transfer the responsibility for employee pension and insurance planning from the employer, union, or government to the employee. It could be argued that an employee might act irresponsibly and squander his earnings. First, that is his right. It is his money. Second, employers, unions, and governments also have a history of squandering these earnings – governments in particular. If an individual squanders his own money it is called "foolishness." If someone else –

like an employer, union, or government – denies an individual control over his own money and then squanders it, it is called "tyranny." So, which is the greater offense – foolishness or tyranny?   Most would agree: tyranny. Responsibility for the employee's well-being is and should remain with the employee. To argue otherwise is to embrace the logic of "*Tellers*" and tyrants.

It also can be argued that few employees have the financial expertise to competently manage these matters for themselves. Very true. However, we can expect many of these individuals to voluntarily – even eagerly – seek out more knowledge in these areas once they have more responsibility in these areas. This is a good thing. Second, it is also true that few employers, union leaders, and government officials have the financial expertise to competently manage these matters. They hire experts, which is exactly what the individual can do as well (for example, financial advisers with insurance and investment firms). However, the difference between personal management of one's own assets and second-party (that is, employer, union, or government) management of one's assets is that the individual is more powerfully motivated to insure the successful management of his own assets than will be a second-party manager who will neither benefit nor suffer from the consequences of his actions.

Conclusion. The proposed plan for payroll and compensation reform is much simpler and makes far more sense than the current system. It would eliminate many immediate problems while avoiding future ones. It would return control of an individual's earnings – all of them, wages and other compensation – to the individual. It would dramatically increase the worker's take-home pay – even to an amount that is well in excess of his current gross pay. It would give the individual a greater opportunity to maximize his return on investment. It would limit the oppressive power of employers, unions, and government while increasing the power of individuals. It would be easier and less expensive to manage. It would relieve all employers – private and public – of the responsibility for pension planning and the consequences thereof. It would solve the looming problem of how to handle the approaching deluge of unfunded liabilities ready to swamp local, state, and federal governmental agencies. It would encourage the entrepreneurial spirit and open significant opportunities for the development of private industry and the creation of jobs. It would end the current complicated, dishonest, and ineffective system while providing a smooth transition to a new and better one.

And one more thing. An increasing number of Americans are becoming outraged by reports of the extremely generous pension plans which many government officials have created for themselves. These pensions often are available for life and after an elected official has served only one term in office. The adoption of the plan described in this chapter would end this. Elected officials, like everyone else, would get a paycheck. What they do with it is up to them; but when the job ends, so too do the paychecks and benefits.

In short, the proposed plan is simple, honest, predictable, and all-American.

Simple. Compensation for labor becomes simple and straight-forward. We eliminate the present complicated system which mixes cash and "in-kind" payments. The employee knows exactly what he is getting and can decide for himself exactly what he wants to do with it. Payroll planning and management for employers would be easy and much less expensive. There would be no need for costly accountants and lawyers to handle payroll-related issues. Business management for small businesses in particular would become much easier, less time-consuming, and less expensive.

Honest. Such a system provides the maximum degree of "transparency." The worker will have a clear and precise knowledge of exactly how much he receives for his labors. Workers will be far less vulnerable and susceptible to manipulation by employers, union officials, and government agents who frequently exploit the confusion created by a complicated system to further their own interests at the expense of the workers.

Predictable. Since this plan eliminates the complications, confusion, and politics from employee compensation, the worker can better perceive and manage not only his present status but his future situation as well. He doesn't need to rely on a disinterested or dishonest second party to explain where he will stand in the future. Control is in his own hands.

All-American. This nation was founded on the belief that each individual has God-given rights to life, property, liberty, and the pursuit of happiness. The present payroll system betrays these values. It denies the worker the **liberty** to **pursue his happiness** and well-being by stealing control over the **property** which he earned and which he needs to manage some of the most critical areas of his **life**. It denies individual workers the freedom to control their own destiny. This destiny has been entrusted to others; and the current disaster confronting the nation testifies to how poorly that decision has played out. America is all about breaking the chains of bondage, not forging those chains. Our success in the future depends upon our determination to return to the values of the past. The time has come to rise up and put down those who enslave us. Tyrants – beware!

CHAPTER ELEVEN

THE STRAIGHT JACKET CHRONICLES; BUREAUCRATIC AND BUDGET REFORM

November 15, 1976. Buried among all the election news in that particular issue of *Business Week Magazine* was an op-ed piece entitled, "Why Bureaucracy Keeps Growing," written by an obscure author. I raced to a nearby magazine stand on the day this edition came out and purchased several copies. Why? Because I was the obscure author, and this was my first article in a prominent, national magazine. Too bad it got buried. Maybe if someone other than a handful of friends and family had read it and taken it to heart, I might not have to write this chapter.

The problems associated with our burgeoning bureaucracies was a big issue back then. It's an even bigger issue now, but it doesn't seem to bother us as much as it used to. Just like many of us have gotten used to our wrinkles, age spots, and clogging arteries, we also seem to have grown quite accustomed to living in the shadow and under the thumb of big bureaucracies. Despite this, they remain a significant threat to our freedoms and future. They are not only symptomatic of our misguided form of government, they are a major factor in the sick symbiosis that perpetuates it. Accordingly, I do have to write this chapter because we have to do something about this problem.

The term "bureaucracy" refers to the departments, agencies, and offices which carry out the functions of government. In effect, bureaucracies comprise the various systems which keep the ship of state sailing along, and the bureaucrats are the crew members. The best way to avoid the problems of big bureaucracies is to reject the philosophy and practice of big government. You don't need as many systems nor crewmen to keep a canoe afloat as you do to keep the Titanic steaming along.

We will always have overgrown bureaucracies as long as we have overgrown government. Big governments need big bureaucracies to do their work. That seems obvious. What is less obvious is the fact that big bureaucracies also need big government to fund, fuel, and facilitate them. Accordingly, bureaucrats can routinely be expected to support big government and will be inclined to sabotage efforts to streamline it.

If you ever have had to deal with some government agency, then you are probably already quite familiar with the problems inherent in bureaucracy. Still, let us invest a few minutes to explore the heart and soul of the bureaucratic mentality and methodology before we offer a couple of simple ways to keep them under control.

Bureaucrats and *"Tellers"* (mentioned earlier in the book) are best friends and eager co-conspirators. *Tellers* seek to dictate and control behavior, and the bureaucrats are their willing tools. *Tellers* require extensive and detailed rules to regulate behavior. The bureaucratic mentality is characterized by a groveling devotion to the development of such rules and to their precise application. It's a marriage made in purgatory, and the consummation of this union spells nothing but trouble for a free people and a vibrant economy – because ultimately, we are the ones who get "consummated." Let us briefly see why.

The bureaucratic mentality and mode of operation conspire to complicate and frustrate the lives and work of productive people and businesses. The bureaucratic mentality is neither adventurous nor courageous. It seeks security rather than opportunity. For this reason, it is inclined to become regulation-bound. It loves rules because there is certainty and apparent safety in rules. Rules add structure to life and relieve a person from the discomfort of having to think. There is no need to ponder the best way to solve a problem when we have a rulebook. The "answer" is already given. The fact that the "answer" may not actually provide a solution doesn't really matter to the bureaucrat. What the "answer" does provide is a pre-determined, no-thought-required way of dealing with situations. It also relieves the bureaucrat from any responsibility for his actions because his only duty is to enforce the rules – whether those rules are any good or not. The sad fact is that the "one-size-fits-all" nature of the rules means that they are often not the best way – nor even a good way – of solving a problem. Ah, but finding solutions is beyond the pay grade of the bureaucrat. His only obligation is to explain the rule and then play god if you should be so rebellious as to "do it some other way" – even if "some other way" is vastly superior to the official way. You see, to the bureaucratic mentality, the goal is not to get the job done. The goal is **how** you attempt to get the job done. And he really isn't too concerned if "how" you get the job done actually works. You see, he doesn't get paid for getting the job done, so he really doesn't care if you get it done or not.

Creativity, initiative, and risk-taking are essential characteristics to the entrepreneurial spirit and a lively economy; but they are anathema to bureaucrats and bureaucracies. Whereas thinking and acting "outside the box" is a prerequisite for innovation and growth, thinking and acting "inside the box" is a necessary mandate of the bureaucratic mentality and methodology. Innovation is simply too risky for the bureaucrat. Accordingly, bureaucracy and innovation are forever at odds. And since innovation is the heart and soul of an enlightened, creative society and a vibrant economy, it is clear that big bureaucracies are destined to be the enemy of an enlightened society and a vibrant economy. I wrote earlier that bureaucracies comprise the various systems which keep the ship of state sailing along. True, but the main effect of a bureaucracy on the economy of a nation is to serve as an anchor which slows it down and threatens to drag it under. Since the wealth of a nation is generated by its economy, it should be obvious that it is in the economic best interests of a nation to keep its bureaucracies weak and tightly constrained. Let us now consider two simple ways to limit bureaucracies and their harmful effects on a society.

The most fundamental thing we can do is to change our regulatory philosophy from one that is "prevention oriented" to one that is "performance oriented." This means that we need to stop telling people and businesses what to do (which *Tellers* and bureaucrats dearly love) and start telling them what to achieve. I know that isn't very illustrative, so allow me to illustrate.

Modern-day bureaucracies, at all levels of government, issue tomes of regulations dictating the most measly mites of minutia imaginable. They know the objectives they want to accomplish and try to slam the door on any escape routes available to scofflaws. That's understandable. People will try to cheat. However, in their obsessed quest to deny even the slightest variation from their intended goals, they design and impose a straight-jacket so confining that it strangulates the ones who have to wear it. And since the ones who have to wear it are we the people trying to pursue our happiness and we the businessmen trying to augment the wealth of we the people, well, it just doesn't have a very happy ending. Allow me to regale you with three examples taken from my time in straightjackets.

A number of years ago I decided to renovate some commercial properties that I own. By doing this I would help beautify my part of the city while, hopefully, insuring a more dependable income stream in the future. Of course, this required me to lie directly across the regulatory railroad tracks of the building and planning department and expose myself to the very real danger of being flattened by the locomotive of the civil service. I knew that it wasn't so much a matter of **if** this would happen but rather of **when** and **how often** it would happen. One of the "whens" was when my general contractor called to tell me that he was going to have to reset a toilet. Now, that doesn't seem like such a demanding task that a general contractor would feel obligated to inform his employer; but any bureaucrat worth his salt can make eating an ice cream cone a frustrating and expensive task. You don't even want to consider what one could do with a toilet – but we will anyway.

Handicap regulations require that the center of the floor drain for toilets be at least eighteen inches from the nearest wall. The officious inspector who was dispatched to my job site in order to keep the world safe from deviants discovered a delinquent john that was offset a mere seventeen-and-a-half inches. Does anyone really think that a scant half-inch would render the facility unusable to a handicapped person? Didn't matter. Strict compliance is the only option – which, I guess, means that there is no option, only a dictate. I watched as the contractor removed the toilet, broke up the floor tile – which had the exact skid coefficient required by the regulations – jackhammered the concrete around the drain, and scootchied the drain pipe over a half-inch with a wrecking bar. He then re-poured the concrete, re-tiled the floor, and re-set the toilet. Good thing he did, too, because in the intervening years there have been exactly zero handicapped persons who have used that toilet. So glad I could be of help.

Example Two. The owner of an established business in town wanted to move to my location for various reasons, the most pressing of which was an unconscientious landlord who wasn't taking care of his business. Everything was arranged, the first check was written, and the signed lease was about to be delivered when the new tenant decided that he should visit our friends at building and planning to insure that there weren't any unforeseen problems with the move. Well, there were. They told him he couldn't do it. Why? Because I didn't have enough parking spaces. In the first place, who are they to tell him what he needs in order to run a successful business? He had been doing this for years, so I think we can surmise that he knows how much parking he needs. But, no. The city had a "formula" that had been devised by genuine bureaucrats whose wisdom, of course, exceeded that of someone who actually knew what he was doing. Ah, but there is more – and here again we see the fawning devotion to those most measly mites of minutia imaginable mentioned above. I actually compared the number of parking spaces available at my location with the tenant's previous location. I found that I did have less parking available – to be exact, four-tenths of one parking space less. Good thing the city caught that one. We could have witnessed a catastrophe of unspeakable proportions. (In case the reader is wondering what happened, I went to City Hall and had a "talk" with the nice folks at building and planning. My new tenant moved in without delay. Oh, yes, you can beat City Hall. I do it all the time.)

Example Three. This is actually a spinoff from Example Two. In the course of checking into the above tenant's request to relocate, the building and planning clerk discovered that there was a church worshipping in one of my spaces. Well, we can't have that kind of thing going on in the city limits, so our friends in the building and planning department locked and loaded one of their primary harassment weapons – the "Conditional Use Permit." A threatening letter was sent to the operators of the church telling them that they would have to apply for a Development Permit to see if they would even be allowed to stay. The cost: over $7,200. The people who ran the church didn't see the purpose for such a permit – nor could they afford it – so they called me. I called our dutiful bureaucrats at building and planning and asked, among other things, what we would get for $7,200. I was told that the city would have to conduct an analysis of traffic patterns to determine whether having a church at this location would pose a threat to public safety. I asked if there had been any problems or complaints in the area. The clerk checked and said "No." I said, "Well, we're in luck.

The church has been operating at this location for two-and-a-half years with no problems. It looks like we have conducted the study for you. I'll tell you what. I'll only charge you $5,000 for the findings. I just saved the city over $2,000!" The clerk wasn't amused, but the church continues to operate, and it didn't cost them a penny.

These are just three of the many absurd and abusive incidents I have experienced at the hands of just one local bureaucracy. Multiply this times millions and you start to get an idea of the waste and misery perpetrated against the citizenry by our various government agencies across the land. Also keep in mind that we the people get to pay for the whip that is used to torment us.

At the heart of much of this mischief is what I call the "*prevention-oriented*" regulatory philosophy. When we change this operating system, we drastically reduce both the misery and the cost imposed by runaway bureaucracies.

So, what is the "prevention-oriented" regulatory philosophy? It has two basic premises. First, we expect things to go wrong. Very prudent. Second, we believe that we can prevent these things from going wrong by trying to imagine every possible eventuality which could lead to a problem and then writing a rule to prevent it. Very imprudent. Oh, it sounds like a good idea, but it would only work in some fantasized, utopian society. In the real world it creates far more problems than it solves and confines our most creative and productive members within paper prisons and regulatory straightjackets. The "prevention-oriented" operating system is so preoccupied with what we cannot do that it precludes much of what we can do.

I know that most lawyers will disagree with my objections to this approach. They will tell us that such detailed regulations are necessary to be able to prevent or prosecute violators; but we all know that lawyers also tend to be a big part of the problem, so let's not listen to them. Let's listen to reason, and reason demands that we come up with a different approach to regulation. What is this different approach? We need to adopt a "*performance-oriented*" regulatory philosophy.

Under a "prevention-oriented" approach we tell people and businesses what to do – like installing toilets a precise distance from the wall or providing some specified number of parking spaces for a store. Under a "performance-oriented" approach we tell people and businesses what to achieve – like reasonable access to your facilities by handicapped people or sufficient parking to prevent an unsafe situation. Under the "performance-oriented" approach, we simply tell people what we expect them to do then leave them alone as long as they are doing it. We don't assume that there is only one way to accomplish a goal, and we certainly don't assume that some book-trained, inexperienced bureaucrat knows better how to accomplish the goal than someone who actually does it for a living.

What about enforcement? Under a "prevention-oriented" system enforcement is often applied before the problem arises. We tell people, "You can't do it that way." Again, this sounds prudent, but in practice it outlaws many perfectly good ways to accomplish a goal and limits our creativity as a society to the often very limited imaginations of our bureaucrats. Our society and economy are painted in a few shades of gray instead of enabling all the hues of the rainbow to be applied to the canvas. With a "performance-oriented" system, enforcement and punishment is applied after a violation has taken place. Isn't that what we do with other violators? After all, we don't arrest someone because we think he is going to rob a bank, so why do we confine a businessman because we think he might deny a handicapped person the opportunity to use a toilet?

Under the "performance-oriented" approach, we define what is a problem (like causing traffic to be restricted by a certain degree for a particular period of time more than "X" occurrences a year) or what is an objective (like making reasonable provisions for handicapped people to use a toilet) and then say we will punish you thusly if you fail. This is what is meant by "performance-oriented" standards – regulators define what types of performance are acceptable and which are not acceptable and then respond to the consequences. Under the "prevention-oriented" approach, we expect that everyone will fail without the help of government so we minutely define and describe those behaviors which will be allowed. Under the "prevention-oriented" method, punishment is anticipatory – it is imposed before the offense is committed.

Under the "performance-oriented" method, punishment is consequential – it is meted out only after an offense is committed. It is true that the "prevention-oriented" approach will keep many offenses from being committed in the first place, but this is accomplished by punishing everybody in expectation of the offense. It's like preventing bank robberies by arresting everyone before a bank is ever robbed. You'll have a great law-enforcement record, but at the expense of grave injustice and general misery.

I realize that the "performance-oriented" approach is not perfect – but then, what is? I confidently assert, however, that our society will be far more innovative, productive, wealthy, free, and happy by applying this philosophy than by continuing with the "prevention-oriented" approach. I also realize that merely making this recommendation will drive our "*Tellers*", bureaucrats, and lawyers up a wall, but better them than us.

Adopting "performance-oriented" standards for regulations is absolutely essential in order to end the crippling effects of the "prevention-oriented" approach which is commonplace today. Still, we have reason to believe that the results of such a change in regulatory philosophy may not be long-lived. Why? Because the bureaucrats themselves will have an incentive to sabotage it. They have a pretty good thing going for themselves and they won't want to lose it. This, in part, is why so many past attempts at bureaucratic reform have failed. They also fail because there is a natural energy within bureaucracies which causes them to grow larger as well as increasingly expensive and inefficient. Even a sincere government official who genuinely seeks to reform this system will eventually wear out, much like a salmon who always has to swim upstream. So, is it realistic to expect that we can accomplish lasting bureaucratic reform? Sure. All we have to do is change the energy within the system. In other words, change the direction of the stream so the salmon – or the reforming government official – can go with the flow instead of against it. So, how do we do this?

We must elect bold, courageous government executives – like city mayors, county supervisors, state governors, and a national president – who pledge to undertake the following measures and then do it.

First, he promises to audit every governmental agency and office under his authority to find and end waste and inefficiency. Yeah, yeah, we've all heard that before, and it never seems to get to the implementation phase. True, but it still is an essential aspect of effective management, and we the people must insist on implementation. But while we're waiting....

Second, the chief executive announces that there will be an immediate ten percent cut in the budgets of all government agencies and offices. It's probably a pretty safe bet that virtually every department of government is wasting at least ten percent of its budget. But in the rare instances where this may not be the case, the wise chief executive offers an exemption.

Third, the heads of the government agencies and offices experiencing these cuts may appeal this action if they feel that the vital interests of the people will be jeopardized by this ten percent reduction. Their agency or office will then go to the head of the list to be audited. If the auditors determine that the vital interests of the people will not be jeopardized by the cut, then punitive actions will be taken against the agency or office as well as against the department head who filed the appeal. Any office which loses the appeal will be assessed an additional three percent cut in its budget, and the department head will be subject to dismissal or demotion at the discretion of the chief executive. This will likely preclude frivolous appeals which waste time and money. If a department head realizes that he will play "You Bet Your Job" should he make such an appeal, we can rest assured that there won't be very many of them. By the way, the "vital interests of the people" will be defined in terms of the loss of lives, jobs, health, and homes. Some bug losing its cozy habitat, some welfare queen losing her free cell phone, or some welfare king being unable to buy another tattoo do not qualify as "vital interests."

These three measures together will have a significant effect on the size and expense of bureaucracies, but they will do nothing to change the energy of the situation. We'll just tick-off a bunch of bureaucrats who will look for every opportunity to sabotage the operation. Something else remains to be done.

Fourth, we take a page from the private sector's book and give the bureaucrats the opportunity to line their pockets through the public sector's equivalent of profit sharing. We agree to let the bureaucrats keep a portion of any savings they come up with over and above the ten percent cut. Here's how it works. Let's say there are five hundred people working in some state agency. Let's say the state government agrees to split any savings in addition to the ten percent cut between the bureaucrats who find the savings and the people of the state on a 50 - 50 basis. Let's say that the workers in this particular agency collectively find an additional two million dollars of savings over the course of a year. Half (one million dollars) is returned to the people of the state and the other half is shared equally among all the workers in that department. That would be a two thousand dollar bonus for each bureaucrat just for doing his job more efficiently. Now, this **will** change the energy within bureaucracies. We will create an army of whistle-blowers and cost-cutters who are looking for savings around every corner and under every rock because they will get to share in those savings. "Hey, boss. We can save fifty-one cents per ream if we buy our paper from *Office Wizard* instead of *Office Guru!*" "Hey, boss. How come we keep giving away retractable pens with our department name printed on them in florescent ink? Let the people get their own pens!" "Hey, boss. Why do we keep buying two-sided, full-color business cards with this funky seal embossed in gold when all we need is name, job, and contact information printed in black ink on white paper?"

Indeed, we will always have overgrown bureaucracies as long as we have overgrown government. The surest and most fundamental way to relieve the people from the cost, waste, and abuse of big bureaucracies is to relieve the people from the philosophy of big government. Decades ago that obscure author advised, "The problem, therefore, lies in a concept of government that knows no bounds. It stems from a theory of unlimited state power and responsibility – from the notion that the state is entitled to interfere everywhere, pursue every social injustice, real or imagined, and champion every cause." True, but we do not have to wait for the adoption of a whole new philosophy of government before achieving relief from the abuses of big bureaucracies. Relief can begin almost immediately through the adoption of "performance-oriented" standards of regulation and through the implementation of our four-part plan to change the energy and reduce the cost of bureaucracies at all levels. The implementation of these reforms themselves will begin the process of shrinking the government. Sometimes the dog is reluctant to wag its tail. In times like these, it just may be necessary for us to grab the tail and shake the dog ourselves.

CHAPTER TWELVE

LINKAGE; TOWARD THE PROPER INTERPRETATION OF THE CONSTITUTION

The Constitution of the United States is a unique and remarkable document. It detailed the framework of a government that would allow a diverse people to unite, aspire, and achieve. The genius and power of this plan lies in the word "allow." The Constitution did not compel the course of the nation; it did not dictate the path of the people. It established a minimal governmental structure to facilitate a civil society, and then it got out of the people's way. It "allowed" them to pursue their happiness. It was written by "*Letters*" not "*Tellers*." In this regard, it truly is rare in human history. In this regard, and only in this regard, did it facilitate the development of history's greatest superpower. You see, it is not governments that make people great. It is people that make nations great. The best thing a government can do is protect the rights of the people, promote the morals that will keep them safe, and then get the hell out of the way.

The awe and reverence with which the Constitution was regarded was well-deserved. To be sure, it was not perfect; but it was so magnificent and mighty that it was able to survive its imperfections and point the way for its own refinement. The only thing it was not mighty enough to survive was the treacherous betrayal of the very people who swore to preserve, protect, and defend it.

Over the decades traitorous *Tellers* and devious deceivers sought to impose their will on the people instead of allowing the will of the people to manifest itself. But always their sinister agenda ran headlong into an unmovable obstacle: the Constitution, the faithful defender of the people's rights and liberties. Unwilling to accept a well-deserved defeat, the *Tellers* and deceivers developed a new strategy. If you can't beat it, redefine it. And so they did. While pretending to honor the Constitution, they engaged in a deliberate effort to deform and distort, to misrepresent, misinterpret, and mangle its original intent. Like a Halloween pumpkin being transformed by the hands of some fiendish ghoul, the outer shell appears much the same as before, but it has been gutted, and a new face is being carved into the hollow husk.

The Constitution is dead. Behold the prize hanging on the hunter's wall. It may look like a deer, but it is lifeless. It can do none of the things that the deer could do when it was alive. It has been reduced to a trophy, and so, too, has the Constitution. It has become a taxidermied monstrosity, and we are living in a post-Constitutional period.

Jefferson anticipated this. He once wrote, "The Constitution ... is a mere thing of wax in the hands of the judiciary, which they may twist and shape into any form they please." The twisted reshaping of the Constitution has now proceeded so long that, in fact, the Constitution no longer governs us. It is gone – replaced by a malignant perversion that is used to abuse our rights and liberties instead of protecting them. If we the people allow this to continue – if we fail to reestablish the Constitution – the inevitable consequence must be the death of history's noblest nation and the dousing of liberty's light.

We must return the Constitution to the throne and then surround it with a solid bulwark to guard it into the future. To accomplish this, we must develop a faithful standard through which the Constitution can be properly understood, interpreted, and applied. That concept, that standard, that bulwark, is "*Linkage.*"

To understand and define Linkage, we must begin at a strange place, with what may seem like a peculiar admission: The Constitution is **not** our nation's founding document. It cannot be. It was written eleven years after the founding of our country. The establishing document of the United States is the Declaration of Independence, and this is where we begin to build our bulwark. This is the crucible from which we will forge the solid steel of Linkage.

As was pointed out in Chapter Six, the Founders presented a very concise but profound philosophy of government in the Declaration. They felt compelled to do so. After all, they were arguing that they were entitled to separate themselves from Great Britain because the British government had become illegitimate – that it had violated the most solemn and sacred responsibility of any government. Well, if one is going to claim that something is illegitimate, one had better be prepared to define what is legitimate. The Founders did precisely that in the second paragraph of the Declaration.

> *We hold these truths to be self-evident, that all men are created equal, that they are endowed by their Creator with certain unalienable Rights, that among these are Life, Liberty and the pursuit of Happiness. That to secure these rights, Governments are instituted among Men, deriving their just powers from the consent of the governed, That whenever any Form of Government becomes destructive of these ends, it is the Right of the People to alter or to abolish it, and to institute new Government, laying its foundation on such principles and organizing its powers in such form, as to them shall seem most likely to effect their Safety and Happiness.*

Hidden in plain sight is a philosophy of government that almost no one has perceived – at least in recent generations. If I may be allowed to shuffle the verbiage a bit, the core responsibility of government becomes quite obvious – and quite devastating to the agenda of the *Tellers* and deceivers. "Governments are instituted among Men""to secure these rights""that ... are endowed by their Creator."

The proposition of the Declaration is that governments exist to do the work of God. Today's faithless generations may ask, "Which god?," but that would not have been in question during the late eighteenth century. Reasonable estimates contend that well over ninety percent of the Founders were committed Christians, so we can be pretty certain that they were referring to the God of the Bible. (If anyone tells you that they were mostly Deists, ask for proof. There is none. This is a completely unsubstantiated claim that was fostered by the malevolent and spread by the ignorant.) Foremost among a government's responsibilities in accomplishing its work is securing – that is establishing and protecting – the rights of the people. This is so critical and elemental that the people have the right to alter or abolish any government that becomes destructive of these ends either through incompetence or deliberate design.

We discussed this philosophy in more detail in Chapter Six, but this brief synopsis is sufficient for our present purposes. The point is that the Founders clearly stated what they believed to be the proper role of government. So, how does that help us to accurately understand and interpret the Constitution? Because the Constitution was written in order to implement and institutionalize the philosophy of government presented in the Declaration.

Of course it was! This was the philosophy that justified declaring our independence. This was the philosophy for which we mutually pledged our lives, our fortunes, and our sacred honor. We fought for it. We sacrificed for it. We died for it. Do you honestly believe that we are going to forget all about it a mere four years after the Revolution ended? Of the forty men who signed the Constitution, six had signed the Declaration, twenty-three had been veterans of the Revolution, and one had commanded the Continental Army throughout the eight years of the Revolution. I think we can rest assured that these patriots would have fought as hard to enshrine this philosophy in the Constitution as they fought to proclaim it in the Declaration and to accomplish it on the battlefield.

In effect, the Declaration is the spirit of the law. The Constitution represents the letter of the law. And as any good legal scholar or theologian will tell you, the spirit of the law is preeminent to the letter of the law. This means that we cannot accurately interpret and apply the words of the Constitution apart from the Declaration. The two must be linked – hence, "linkage." Whenever the intent or meaning of the Constitution is unclear, we must first view it through the lens of the Declaration.

The Declaration is the telescope through which we can clearly observe the overall purpose of the Constitution. It is the microscope through which we can accurately perceive the wisdom and direction of its finest details. Had we faithfully used that telescope, we never would have allowed an errant concept of "separation of church and state" to remove from government the very God it was supposed to be serving. We never would have allowed a warped understanding of "promote the general welfare" to be twisted so as to allow the violation of fundamental property rights and individual liberties. Had we consistently used that microscope, we never would have given a second thought to some perverse claim regarding a "right" to abortion – which violates the first and foremost right to life. Furthermore, the contention that there is a "right" to same-sex marriage would never have made it even to the county courthouse much less the Supreme Courthouse.

We have suffered grievously because we have allowed the Declaration and the Constitution to become unlinked. We capped the fount of wisdom. We cut ourselves off from the source of our greatness. We chose to look at life through the distorted spyglasses of the charlatans and deceivers and *Tellers* instead of the clear and powerful lens of erudition. Now, we must set things aright.

*   *   *

I groan inwardly as I contemplate writing the next words, for I know that they may be unappreciated by friends and exploited by foes. The task of reestablishing the Constitution will not be easy, it may not be peaceful, and it quite likely will not be Constitutional. It could be all three – easy, peaceful, and Constitutional – and I pray it will; but I strongly suspect that it will not.

Perhaps – perhaps – upon reading these words the people will awaken, perceive the error of their ways, dedicate themselves to resurrecting the Constitution and reestablishing its principles, and then go skipping merrily, hand-in-hand down the yellow brick road singing *Kumbayuh*. Perhaps, but I wouldn't bet on it.

Powerful forces have grown up that know the Constitution is their enemy. Their perceived best interests rely on perpetuating the hollow shell of the Constitution's corpse while idolizing the ghoulish features that have been carved into its remains. The same people who slaughtered the deer now would have us worship the dead head that hangs on their wall. They will not go gently into that good night. Their power, prestige, and prosperity all rely upon keeping their Frankenstein creature alive. On the other hand, the power, prestige, and prosperity of the true United States and its people rely upon destroying this vile creature and resurrecting the real Constitution. There is going to be a fight, but one well worth the effort.

As the movement begins to resurrect and reestablish the Constitution, the Enemy will marshal its forces. It will attempt to cling to power in local, state, and national governments by rallying its loyal constituencies – the *Tellers*, petty tyrants, freeloaders, and ignorant. It will engage in scare-tactics to mobilize them to vote in large numbers; and when that isn't sufficient, it will seek to multiply its actual numbers by harvesting the well-cultivated fields of voter fraud. If they win, we come to the fork in the road, and we must make a dreadful decision.

If we win – if we take back the seats of local, state, and national governments – the Enemy will take to the streets. They will protest and pillage, rebel and riot, loot and plunder; and then they will portray us as monsters whether we allow their rebellion or confront it. And so, we come to the fork in the road, and we must make a dreadful decision.

"History" knows where this will lead, but most Americans do not know their history anymore. The fork in the road is simply this: we follow the current path which can lead nowhere but to the decline and fall of the United States, or we take a different path and be prepared to do whatever is necessary to climb back up the hill and reestablish America the Great.

Whatever is necessary.

"Whatever is necessary" might take many forms, but there is one form in particular that we must specifically address. The tragic irony of our situation is that we may need to pursue unconstitutional methods in order to resurrect the Constitution. On the surface, and to superficial thinkers, this may seem contradictory, hypocritical, and unacceptable. In reality, it is historical and will likely prove inescapable. The unlearned and unsophisticated may demand, "How can you honor the Constitution by violating it!" Perhaps an analogy will help explain and justify.

February, 2000. After experiencing suspicious symptoms for a couple of months, I finally relented and went to my doctor. An angiogram revealed that I had a heart condition which my cardiologist called "The Widowmaker." He explained that I would have a massive, unsurvivable heart attack within the next couple of months, and perhaps as soon as a few days. He scheduled me for open-heart surgery first thing the next morning. Throughout the evening before and the morning of the operation I felt and looked fine. After the operation I looked like death-warmed-over. My wife was brought in to see me immediately after the surgery. She said that after a quick glance, she had to look away because I appeared so ghastly. My condition was critical, and, once I regained consciousness, I really didn't feel very well. This was despite the fact that the operation had gone smoothly and was performed by a brilliant surgeon. He deliberately made me much worse so I would have the chance of becoming much better. The man who took an oath to "do no harm," nearly killed me in order to save me. No one has a problem with that, nor should they. Such is the reality of emergencies. Actions which are completely inappropriate – and likely even illegal and immoral – in routine situations become necessary during dire exigencies. The same logic applies to restoring the Constitution.

The best that we can expect from man-made laws is that they guide us wisely most of the time and minimize the occurrence of emergencies. However, dire situations, disasters, and emergencies will happen; and it is precisely when we need inspired leadership the most that the law is most likely to fail us – even if that law is the Constitution. It is in times such as these that we desperately need exceptional leadership that is willing to rise above the temporary limitations of the law in order to save the law for the long run. This is what Washington did during the Revolution. He did not always honor the principles espoused in the second paragraph of the Declaration. It is a good thing that he did not, or we never would have had the opportunity to establish a government upon them. Lincoln did not always honor the dictates of the Constitution during the Civil War. It is a good thing that he did not, or we never would have been able to preserve a government based upon them. Modern American leaders may not be able to honor the principles of the Constitution during the Second American Revolution. Some day our grandchildren will be able to say, "It is a good thing that they did not, or we never would have had the blessing of living under the Constitution in America the Great."

I realize that violating elements of the Constitution in order to save it is a dangerous proposition; but so is open-heart surgery where the physician brings his patient to the door of death in order to defeat death. These are dangerous words for dangerous times, for they can be used by a potential tyrant to convert potential tyranny into a reality. Still, we haven't left ourselves much choice. I agreed to the risk of possible death during open-heart surgery because my only option was certain death without it. I entrusted my life to the hands of a great surgeon because I knew that – even though he would nearly kill me – I could trust in his commitment to work to restore my health. Similarly, we may have to entrust our national life to the hands of a great leader because we know that – even though he may do violence to the precepts of the Constitution for a short time – we can trust his commitment to work to restore this one nation under God and this one people under the Constitution.

It is far easier to read and react to these words than to accurately contemplate and carry them out. The raw reality is this: when the Enemy responds in force, then we must be prepared to do likewise. God help us – this will be war. This will be the price we must pay for our inattention, indifference, and inaction. We have allowed this to happen; and now we must either stand by and experience the decline of History's noblest nation, or we must stand up and fight for her.

We must stand up and fight for her!

CHAPTER THIRTEEN

DROPPING THE HAMMER; THE CONSTITUTIONAL GOVERNOR

In Chapter Four we likened America's chances for meaningful national reform to the prospects of a combat archer with an empty quiver. He faces certain death. The traditional politics of the traditional politicians in the traditional political parties have proven themselves worse than worthless. The Democratic and Republican Parties have nothing to offer us but more of the same formula for disaster that they have used to bring this great land and its people to the brink of collapse. They speak of hope, but coming from their lips it is nothing more than a clanging gong, a marketing tool, a barren and meaningless propaganda ploy. Theirs is the politics of hopelessness, and any continuing misguided loyalty to them will inevitably end in our ruin.

The future of America lies on a different path from that paved by our party machines. America remains the land of opportunity, but we will have to break free from a slavish devotion to our grandparents' political parties in order to pursue that opportunity. In fact, we need something as new as tomorrow and as vintage as 1776. We need some arrows to put in our quiver.

The last six chapters have provided those arrows – magnificent munitions that can fly straight and true – bold bolts to slay the dragons of hopelessness and oppression while hitting the targets of liberty and opportunity.

Arrow Number One: No Party Affiliation. It used to be argued that the parties served special interests instead of the national interest. Today, their focus has become even more narrow. They betray the national interests while exploiting special interests in order to secure their own interests. We are merely fodder to the parties. Enough! We the people must take back control of our own destinies and relegate the party machines to the graveyard of a dark past.

Arrow Number Two: Tax Reform. The proper role of taxation is to fairly provide the funds necessary to perform the essential functions of government. Those days are long gone in America. Today the major role of taxation is to provide the politicians with the funds they need to buy enough votes to keep themselves in power. The insane proliferation of taxation that we have witnessed in the last century is threatening to strangulate the very economic forces upon which our survival depends. It must end, and the simple four-part program described in Chapter Eight will remove the noose from our necks while fashioning a fitting dog collar with which to restrain our profligate politicians.

Arrow Number Three: Voting Reform. You paid for your home. Would you allow someone who had no ownership of it to decide the house rules? You paid for your car. Would you allow someone who had no ownership of it to determine how it is driven and maintained? You paid for your business. Would you allow someone who had no ownership of it to manage it? Of course not. You just cannot trust people who have no "skin in the game" to play the game responsibly. For the same reason, we need to restrict the power to decide the course of our country to those who have an interest in its outcome **and** who will pay the bill for accomplishing that outcome.

Arrow Number Four: Payroll and Compensation Reform. Money is power. Control the way a worker is paid, and you control the worker. Control the worker and you control the nation. Over the last several decades we have created a payroll system which deprives the worker of control over most of the money he earns – whether in the form of cash or other benefits. Control has been given to the boss, the union, or the government. This system makes the worker a puppet on the stage that he built. It is stealth tyranny, and it can be easily remedied. Simply pay the worker one hundred percent of the money that the employer spends on him, and let the worker decide what to do with his earnings.

Arrow Number Five: Bureaucratic and Budget Reform. The adoption of a big-government philosophy has resulted in the growth of big bureaucracies. Big bureaucracies limit our freedoms and choke off innovation and productivity. We must deal with this problem by changing the regulatory philosophy used by most bureaucracies and by significantly limiting the size and expense of these bureaucracies. We accomplish the first objective by changing from a "prevention-oriented" approach to regulation (where we try to anticipate and preclude every imaginable problem that might arise) to a "performance-oriented" approach (where we establish performance standards and then respond to how individuals and organizations behave). Secondly, we deal with the size and cost of bureaucracies by implementing an immediate, across-the-board, ten percent cut in everyone's budget and then encourage subsequent cost-cutting by sharing savings between the tax-payers and the members of the department which accomplished the savings.

Arrow Number Six: Linkage. Our nation was blessed with a plan of government that established justice, guarded the rights of the people, unleashed their productive energies, promoted their general welfare, protected them from foreign dangers, and propelled them to greatness. Had we only done as much for the Constitution as it has done for us, there would be no need for this book nor the revolution it proposes. But we didn't. We allowed the Constitution to be redefined and desecrated by enemies domestic who had to replace it in order to accomplish their own sinister agenda. The price of reestablishing the Constitution will likely be high; but even after we achieve this goal, the danger of losing it again in future generations will remain unless we create a faithful sentinel to protect it. Fortunately, we do not have to create such a guard. It already exists. We must merely rediscover and apply it. "It" is the Declaration of Independence. The Declaration provides the philosophy of government which the Constitution was designed to implement and institutionalize. Accordingly, we must interpret the Constitution in conjunction with the Declaration. It is only through linking these two documents that we can honor and preserve them both.

Six awesome arrows. Six bold bolts. Our quiver is full, but how do we employ them? True, a combat archer with an empty quiver is a dead man. But it is also true that a combat archer with a full quiver and no bow is equally doomed. So, what is our bow? How do we let fly our arrows?

In the United States it is typical for someone entering a career in the military, law enforcement, or government service to take an oath to preserve, protect, and defend the Constitution of the United States – or words to that effect. It is doubtful if ten percent of the people who take that oath have ever read the Constitution. This does not change the fact that they made a promise and are expected to keep it. An "oath", as it was understood by those who wrote the Constitution, was a promise to God in consideration of the certainty of future rewards and punishments associated with how well they kept that promise.

Most people who make this solemn pledge merely say the words and then go blithely on their way completely oblivious to the solemnity of that pledge. In their minds they merely got their ticket punched allowing them to commence their careers and qualify for a paycheck. For some, however, it was more. Much more. They took their promise seriously. Among these were a handful of sheriffs – the senior elected law-enforcement officers for a county or parish. They realized that their primary duty was not to keep their uniforms smartly pressed and their shoes brightly polished; nor to keep the local politicians happy; nor to keep the people safe; nor even to obey the law. Their preeminent responsibility is to preserve, protect, and defend the Constitution – even if that meant that their shoes might get scuffed, the politicians might get ticked, the people might be less "safe", and certain laws might be ignored – or violated. "Preserve, protect, and defend the Constitution" – that's it! They take their oath seriously, and they call themselves, "Constitutional Sheriffs."

Such sheriffs are Constitutional Heroes – stalwart defenders of our nation's founding principles. They are committed to turning their jurisdictions into havens which secure the blessings of liberty for ourselves and our posterity. The "Constitutional Sheriff" is a power-ful concept, though very limited in scope. But what if it weren't? What if we had more of them? In fact, what if we took the concept to the next level? What if we had a "Constitutional Governor?"

The Constitutional Governor would be vested with tremendous power to quickly right the wrongs of the past and accomplish great good immediately. This is be-cause he will not be playing by the rules of the current game. He will play a different game altogether which will allow him to bypass restrictive and time-consuming procedures.

Given the rules of the current game, what is the like-lihood of reversing and ending those harmful practices that have resulted from erroneous Supreme Court rul-ings? Slim to none. Think about it. First we would need the death or retirement of enough of the wayward jus-tices to create the opportunity to change the ideologi-cal composition of the Court. Then we would need a sitting president who would be inclined to nominate re-placements who would hold the proper values. Next, we would need enough United States Senators to agree with these nominations. All of these factors would have to be realized just to change the composition of the Court. How many years (decades?) would that likely take? And then we would have to wait for just the right case to wind its way through the judicial system to afford the oppor-tunity to secure a new judgment that could reverse the previous wrongful ruling.

Let us look at the effect of just one errant Supreme Court ruling to give us an idea of the high price we will pay if we continue to play by these rules. In 1973 Roe v. Wade legalized abortion in the United States. The philosophy of government professed by the Declaration clearly shows that the government's most solemn and sacred responsibility is to "secure" our rights, and that "life" is the first and foremost right that must be secured. Abortion is a violation of the right to life. Linkage clearly demonstrates that the Constitution must secure – not violate – this right. Accordingly, abortion is absolutely indefensible and the Court's ruling in Roe v. Wade is wrong and must be overturned immediately. The American death toll resulting from this decision is approaching sixty million and counting. By comparison, the killing of 128 Americans aboard the ocean liner Lusitania on May 7, 1915, encouraged this nation to enter World War I nearly two years later. The deaths of 2,402 Americans at Pearl Harbor on December 7, 1941, led us to declare war the very next day. The deaths of 2,996 Americans on September 11, 2001, immediately incited us to launch a war on terror. And yet, over four decades have passed since the Court unleashed genocide on Americans, and up to this date we still have no prospect nor plan for fighting back.

We do now.

A Constitutional Governor who takes his oath seriously and uses linkage to correctly interpret the Constitution can declare war **immediately** on errant Supreme Court decisions as well as on wrongful legislation from both state and national legislative assemblies.

How would this happen? Once the governor becomes aware of a violation of the Constitution, he begins the following process. The governor – honoring his duty to preserve, protect, and defend the Constitution – would declare a particular practice unconstitutional. Let us continue with the example of abortion. He would then justify this determination using Linkage. Having made his case, he declares that he will use the police powers available to him as chief executive of the state to intervene and stop an unconstitutional practice. In this case he would order the cessation of abortion and would use his police power to close all facilities which do not comply. Done. It won't take years. It can be accomplished in hours.

"Oh," you say, "but the 'pro-choice' advocates will not give up so easily." Of course they won't. If they protest peacefully, that is their right. If they protest violently, they will be arrested, indicted, tried, convicted, sentenced, and imprisoned. That is our right. If they take the matter to court, good. We now have Linkage to support our case and overturn the judicial errors of the past. But, what if we don't win in court? What if the case goes to the Supreme Court, and there are sufficient leftovers on the bench to overthrow the action of the Constitutional Governor? Then the time has come for us to overthrow the Court – or, at least those members of it who support a clearly unconstitutional position. Remember, Supreme Court justices also take an oath to preserve, protect, and defend the Constitution of the United States. If they should betray and dishonor that oath to the supreme secular authority of the land – the Constitution – then they have committed treason and must be charged, tried, and punished accordingly.

Others may object that the Supreme Court is the ultimate arbiter of Constitutionality, and, therefore, this proposed course of action is not legitimate. First of all, the Supreme Court, or at least certain members of the Court, are a party to this action. Their wayward rulings are the issue in this case. Since they are, in effect, the defendants, they have an interest in the outcome of this action and must recuse themselves, leaving others who believe in Linkage to make the final decision. Second, many legal luminaries – not the least of which is Thomas Jefferson – have argued that the Supreme Court does not have ultimate authority in all cases. Jefferson wrote, "The Constitution ... meant that its coordinate branches should be checks on each other. But the opinion which gives to the judges the right to decide what laws are constitutional and what not, not only for themselves in their own sphere of action but for the Legislature and Executive also in their spheres, would make the Judiciary a despotic branch." (Letter to Spencer Roane in 1819.) "The Constitution on this hypothesis is a mere thing of wax in the hands of the judiciary, which they may twist and shape into any form they please." (Letter to to Abigail Adams in 1804.)

Finally, the argument that the Supreme Court has the authority to overrule the actions of a Constitutional

Governor assumes that the Constitution in currently in effect. As was argued earlier, it is not. We are living in a post-Constitutional period. Our objective is to reestablish the Constitution, and some methods for accomplishing this may be "extraordinary."

*   *   *

We have referred to six "arrows" and a "bow" for accomplishing dramatic and necessary changes in the United States. The words, "arrow" and "bow," however, are weak analogies. These are thermonuclear devices with unspeakable power to affect change. We must deploy and employ them immediately if we are to have any hope of reestablishing America the Great peacefully. The best way to do this is through the determined actions of courageous Constitutional Sheriffs and Governors. These may well be the colonels and generals of the Second American Revolution – at least, if that revolution is to be a peaceful one. Should no such colonels and generals arise – or if they should fail – then our only hope will be for other generals to step up, and their weapons will not be analogies for arrows, bows, and thermonuclear devices. They will be compelled to use the real thing.

God, help us.

CHAPTER FOURTEEN

THE ANCHOR. THE SAIL; ON EARTH AS IT IS IN HEAVEN

God, help us.

In his first inaugural address on April 30, 1789, George Washington proclaimed, "No people can be bound to acknowledge and adore the Invisible Hand which conducts the affairs of men more than the people of the United States. Every step by which they have advanced to the character of an independent nation seems to have been distinguished by some token of providential agency...." In other words, God helped us.

Washington continued, "We ought to be no less persuaded that the propitious smiles of Heaven can never be expected on a nation that disregards the eternal rules of order and right which Heaven itself has ordained...." In other words, if God does not continue to help us, all will be lost. Unless America blesses God, God will not bless America. If He withdraws His "providential agency," America will fall.

If we get everything else right but leave out God, America will fall. This proposition may be relatively easy for a person of faith to accept; but what about the skeptic and the non-believer? Why should they accept this judgment and the policies which flow from it? Simple. They worked before. Why wouldn't they work again? Besides, if you love liberty, you have no choice. If you do not love liberty, you have no truck with us.

As was pointed out earlier, the philosophy of government which is pronounced in the second paragraph of the Declaration of Independence is that "Governments are instituted among Men" "to secure these rights" "that ... are endowed by their Creator." God is the heart, soul, mind, and strength of this concept. He is the originator of our rights, and His will is the object of good government. This is how – and only how – we can realize blessings on Earth as they are in Heaven. When we stray from our commitment to Him, we abandon all hope of receiving His blessings. The Founders knew this, and they wove this commitment into the very fabric of their new nation.

The essence of the "American Way" is the preservation of rights; in particular, life, property, and liberty. God is the author of life and the creator of property. He will not allow us to abuse His creation with impunity. And as for liberty, well, without a reverence for and obedience to God, liberty will not long survive. It cannot.

Back in Chapter Two I argued what the Founders understood: liberty cannot exist outside of a moral society. That is not an unsubstantiated claim by a religious kook. It is a rock-hard historic inevitability. Allow me to briefly repeat a summary of the argument presented in Chapter Two. The nature of immorality is pernicious selfishness. A nation of immoral people pursuing their selfish interests leads to unbounded miseries and chaos. The population will not long tolerate this condition and will turn to a strongman who can restore order and safety. Liberty is exchanged for security, and tyranny prevails. On the other hand, a moral population disciplines itself. When morality prevails, the inner policeman maintains order and the society needs neither so many external policemen nor tyrants to maintain order and safety.

If you love liberty, then you must secure morality; and morality is not man-made. The moral philosophies of man are but fleeting opinions – shifting sands which provide no basis for enduring structures. The wisdom of God, on the other hand, furnishes a solid rock upon which individual and national lives can be built. The Tree of Liberty only survives in moral soil, and that is the creation of the Creator.

Our plan of government can only work and survive among a moral populace. John Adams – first Vice-president, second President, and one of the men who understood the underpinnings of that plan of government best – stated as much. "Our Constitution was made only for a moral and religious people. It is wholly inadequate to the government of any other."

America – the bastion and champion of liberty – was built upon the solid rock of Scripture. Despite what fools and traitors may assert, this **is** a Christian nation; and if America ever ceases to be a Christian nation, America will cease to be. God has personally shepherded every step by which we have advanced to the character of an independent, prosperous, and powerful nation. He guided Pilgrims across angry seas and established them to mentor a pristine continent. He inspired a simple but honest folk to treasure liberty, righteousness, and justice. He inflamed them with a passion to stand resolute against tyrants, and He granted them the power to prevail – again and again and again. He illuminated a pathway for them to grow and to become a light for themselves and for others cowering in the dark corners of a wretched planet. He blessed them with riches – for themselves and to share with others. He sanctified them for His purposes and bestowed upon them a mantle to go and make disciples. Though our footsteps occasionally faltered, we repented, we turned from our wicked ways, we recommitted to His ways, and He was gracious.

But it is different now. This is not a misstep. We have deliberately run from Him. We have consciously pursued wicked ways. We have cast off His mantle and trod it under foot. In the face of such rebellion, we cannot expect Him to remain patient nor gracious much longer.

But there is still hope – true hope, not the tawdry marketing ploy of deceitful politicians.

"If My people who are called by My name will humble themselves, and pray and seek My face, and turn from their wicked ways, then I will hear from heaven, and will forgive their sin and heal their land." Second Chronicles, 7:14.

We must remember what the first Americans could never forget: That "Every step by which [we] have advanced to the character of an independent nation seems to have been distinguished by some token of providential agency.... We ought to be no less persuaded that the propitious smiles of Heaven can never be expected on a nation that disregards the eternal rules of order and right which Heaven itself has ordained...."

God is the anchor which holds us fast throughout the storms of the ages. He is the sail which propels us into a glorious future. With Him we win. Without Him even disaster will seem benign.

*   *   *

So, how do we accomplish this revival? Leadership – but nor political. Pastoral.

Charles Finney was one of the luminaries of the Second Great Awakening in America during the late Eighteenth Century and early Nineteenth Century. With amazing insightfulness he once remarked, "If there is a decay of conscience, the pulpit is responsible for it. If the public press lacks moral discernment, the pulpit is responsible for it. If the church is degenerate and worldly, the pulpit is responsible for it. If the world loses its interest in Christianity, the pulpit is responsible for it. If Satan rules in our halls of legislation, the pulpit is responsible for it. If our politics become so corrupt that the very foundations of our government are ready to fall away, the pulpit is responsible for it."

Our pastors used to be among the most fearsome and fearless crusaders for the ideals of America. Many were instrumental in fomenting the fires of revolution against the oppression of Great Britain before and during the American Revolution. Their efforts were so devastating to the Royalist cause that the British came to refer to them as the Black Robes Regiment. This is why the Redcoats burned so many churches. And mind you, the pastors did not relegate themselves to the pulpit. Many hung up their clerical robes to don uniforms in the Continental Army – and not as chaplains, but as commanders of assault units and as trigger-pullers.

What has happened? The pastors of yesteryear would be ashamed to share a common cup of communion with today's limp and pusillanimous denizens of the pulpit. There are a few bold ones – a few. But most seem more fearful of losing their tax-exempt status or alienating a few wayward members of their flock than they are the fires of hell. They would be well-advised to remember Christ's judgement against the church of Laodicea, "I know your works, that you are neither cold nor hot. I could wish you were cold or hot. So then, because you are lukewarm, and neither cold nor hot, I will vomit you out of My mouth."

Pastors, you must find the courage and passion to stand again for God and God's America. Remember, you are held to a higher standard. It will not go well for you if you allow an entire nation – especially God's anointed – to collapse and fall to His enemy.

You want to save souls? How about the soul of a nation! You say you don't like politics? So what! You don't like Satan either, and yet it is in the field of politics and government that he does some of his greatest works. This has always been true. This is where the battle is being fought, but you don't like the venue! Well then, guess who wins. And you will have to answer for it. Not to me. Not to them. To Him. So, you had better either prepare your apologies or prepare to fight. How will you be greeted when your time here is over? "Well done, good and faithful servant", or "I vomit you out of My mouth?"

If the Christian community were to honor Scripture, unite, and arise – we win. It's just that simple. No waiting. No violence. Just a glorious victory. This is your task and your responsibility, pastors. If you are not willing to assume that responsibility, then remove your robes, step down, and take a seat. Someone else needs to be in the pulpit, and you need to listen to them.

*   *   *

Yes, even if we get everything else right but leave out God, America will fall. Even if we make manifold errors but stay with God, America will arise. America, restore your relationship with God, reclaim your power, and resume your rightful role: anointed of the Holy One.

The most necessary and powerful element of the Second American Revolution must be this: Vaya con Dios. Go with God. Otherwise, we all will go to hell.

PART THREE

A HISTORY OF THE FUTURE

CHAPTER FIFTEEN

IF YOU CAN KEEP IT.

Dr. James McHenry, a Maryland delegate to the Constitutional Convention of 1787, relates the story of an encounter that happened as he and Benjamin Franklin left Independence Hall on the final day of the Convention. A woman approached and asked Franklin, "Well, Doctor, what have we got – a republic or a monarchy?" Without hesitation Franklin replied, "A republic, if you can keep it."

When the work of the Constitutional Convention was completed, the work of "we the people" began. The establishment of a republic was a historic rarity. It was the result of nothing less than a Providential combination of brilliant political philosophers, dedicated statesmen, courageous warriors, unequalled stamina, magnanimous sacrifices, and much blood. The preservation of that republic would require at least as much. It still does. The question is this: Do we still have what it takes? Can we keep it?

America is fast approaching a fork in the road. Should she continue on her current course, her collapse is certain.

This is not a prediction. It is a pronouncement. This is not some sad suspicion; it is a historic inevitability. There are certain "life forces" which are necessary to maintain the survival of an organism. A trained and experienced physician knows when a tipping point has been reached and life can no longer be sustained. The same is true for organizations – like nations. A good student of social "life forces" will also recognize the portents of decline and death. Should we fail to alter our course quickly, our collapse is a certainty. The only thing uncertain about this is whether the collapse will be sudden and catastrophic or more gradual. There simply are too many variables at work to reliably predict this.

Once we have embarked upon the path that results in collapse, the only option for reestablishing America the Great will be violence, and likely lots of it. This will not be a Second American Revolution. It will be a Second Civil War. The liberty-lovers and the productives will be pitted against the despots and the unproductives. It will be *Letters* versus *Tellers*. It will be hard-working versus hardly-working. Everything will be at stake, and the opposing sides will fight like it. The liberty-lovers and the productives will be fighting for Old America where they can pursue their happiness and enjoy the fruits of their labors. The despots and the unproductives will be fighting for Old Serfdom where they can steal the fruits of other's labors, and the few can exercise dominion over the many.

Collapse or civil war. These will be our only choices once we come to the fork. But we are not there yet. Not quite. There is still time and opportunity to avoid this dire dilemma. But make no mistake about it: our current choices are not much better. We have allowed ourselves to slip into a position from which there is no easy rescue and recovery. Still, our current options are greatly to be preferred to those south of the fork, and I desperately implore you to muster the courage to do what needs to be done, and to do it now.

How will this transpire? How can we employ and deploy the bow and arrows described in the second section of this book in order to begin and win the Second American Revolution? It will not – it cannot happen the way you may suspect. The answer does not lie in taking control of the national capital. The answer lies in taking control of the state capitals. Washington will not lead this revolution. It is too deeply entrenched in the ways of woe to guide us to the promised land. D. C. will prove virtually irrelevant to the Second American Revolution, except in its attempts to obstruct it.

We need just one state to embrace and implement the principles of AR2 in order to begin the Revolution – to fire the next, "shot heard 'round the world." This state will establish the beachhead for follow-on forces. It will receive the honor of being the "First State" of the Second Republic. Preferably, this will be a large and populous state with sufficient impact to maximize and quicken the pace of the Revolution.

The first step is to elect a courageous, uncompromising Constitutional Governor. Ideally, the state's legislature will also be controlled by Revolutionaries, but even this is not necessary. The bold Constitutional Governor will be able to initiate the process himself.

Using Linkage he declares abortion unconstitutional. It clearly is a violation of the first right to life. He uses the police powers available to him to shut down every abortion clinic and stop all abortions performed in hospitals except those absolutely necessary to save the life of the mother – which are extremely rare.

Using Linkage he declares that there is no "right" to same-sex "marriage" and this perverse practice is prohibited. In these two actions he takes huge strides to reestablish the traditional moral foundation which is the basis of a free nation. John Quincey Adams, sixth president of the United States, observed that the American Revolution had "connected in one indissoluble bond, principles of civil government to the principles of Christianity." The Second American Revolution must do likewise.

The Constitutional Governor will also proclaim certain state and federal laws restricting Second Amendment rights to be unconstitutional. Until those laws can be changed by the legislature, he orders a blanket pardon to everyone – individuals, businesses, and other organizations – which have violated or will violate those statutes. Although this will not change the anti-gun rights laws, it will render them null and void. Furthermore, it will quickly stop future state-sponsored oppression as regards our gun rights. What district attorney will commit the scarce resources of personnel, money, and time to prosecute cases when he knows all his efforts will be vacated the moment the gavel hits the judge's bench? And should there be such contrary crusaders in the cause of disarming our people and rendering them defenseless against criminals, terrorists, and tyrants, he will have a hard time getting reelected when a future opponent points out his waste of taxpayer funds.

Next comes the bombshell which will shatter the bulwark of the Marxist-Progressive fortress and create the energy which will propel the Revolution to other states all across the land. The Constitutional Governor declares that it is a violation of property rights to seize one person's property (in the form of money) in order to redistribute that property to others merely to buy their votes. Accordingly, he orders that no more tax dollars will be used to support these practices. Consider the daisy-chain of events which will follow. The unproductive will be faced with two choices: get a job and become productive or leave the state in search of greener pastures. Either way, the people of the "First State" benefit. Unproductives turned productives will now be adding to instead of taking from the wealth of the state. Those who leave will cease to be a drag on that state's economy. And since many of these freeloaders also engage in various criminal activities – from graffiti to theft, from rape to murder – the state will become a safer and happier place to live.

Such an economic policy – especially when combined with the regulatory reform detailed in Chapter Eleven –

will have a profoundly beneficial impact on the First State and provide a powerful incentive for other states to follow. The tax burden will drop substantially. People can keep more of their hard-earned money. The business environment will improve greatly. Productivity, wealth-creation, employment, and wages will soar. The people will enjoy happier and safer lives. Liberty will abound. Furthermore, people and businesses in other states will quickly see the benefits of living in the First State. An exodus of the best people and businesses will begin as more and more pick up stakes to move to the First State. This will bless the First State but doubly curse the others. First, they will lose their best citizens and weaken their tax base. Second, some of the freeloaders abandoning the First State will be coming to the other states seeking their more generous welfare programs. This double-barreled blast will encourage other states to follow the example of the First State or suffer grievous consequences. More and more states join the Revolution. Before long, only a few of the most virulent Marxist-Progressive states will remain. They will become the last refuge of the unproductives. These few holdout states will become veritable cesspools inhabited by benefit-grubbing freeloaders, criminals, and the politicians who built their careers trying to tear down America the Great. Those last remaining states will either have to join the Revolution and follow the example of the First State or collapse under the weight of their miserable Marxist misconceptions.

The Revolution will be complete. Almost. The re-freshed, revitalized, revolutionized nation will then send new representatives to Washington who will clean out the last pocket of resistance: the federal government.

*   *   *

In the next chapter I will offer a history of the future – a description of how the Second Revolution can be fought and won. But God help us if someone else in years to come will have to write a different account, for it will be offered to a world that has lost History's noblest nation.

NOTE: Many specifics of the "future history" de-scribed in the next chapter are impossible to predict. For example, I have given the honor of commencing the Revolution to my home state of California – and surely, it will have the opportunity to claim that honor. However, should the Golden State fail to seize the day, then the honor is up for grabs; and I will be profoundly grateful to whichever state initiates AR2. The reader is advised to heed the general outline for the Revolution rather than be overly concerned about the details.

CHAPTER SIXTEEN

THE NEXT SHOT HEARD 'ROUND THE WORLD

Darkness and desperation had spread across the land and among the people. The light of Liberty was flickering and close to being extinguished. The battle cry of the First American Revolution, "Give me liberty, or give me death!" was nigh unto forgotten. Instead, the death of Liberty itself was fast approaching. We the people had been seduced by the siren song of deceitful politicians and the "useful idiots" who were their water bearers. We had traded freedom for security and had achieved neither.

The morals of the nation – that solid and true foundation upon which every free and prosperous society must be established – were being systematically attacked and attritted. God was exiled from the public arena. The sanctity of life was overruled for the sake of convenience. Christianity was portrayed as the refuge of the simple-minded. The family was being undermined by a welfare system that tore it apart and an entertainment industry which mocked it. Parents were being denied the power to raise up their own children. The public school system preempted the parents' authority and wishes while a system of "Child Protective Services" often exploited flimsy justifications in order to seize children and consign them to abusive foster guardians. The holy institution of marriage was desecrated and shattered by easy divorce and unholy redefinitions.

Political and economic power had been accumulated and aggregated by a wicked Cartel consisting of big political parties, big businesses, big unions, and big bankers. The consequence was big trouble for the people who were fast losing control over nearly every aspect of their lives as well as the power to do much about it.

The Cartel had successfully infiltrated every element of the society that influenced the formation of public opinion. Education, entertainment, the media, publishing, the arts, and even seminaries had become instruments for the propagation of propaganda. The people were conditioned to think and act inside of "boxes" that had been skillfully designed by the box makers to keep them under control. They had nearly lost the ability for critical and original thought. Though aware of grievous problems, they could imagine no other "solutions" than to continue the same, sick policies that had created the grievous problems in the first place. Malaise and then depression overcame the people as they lost hope of finding any way out. Reform-minded individuals and organizations lost heart and retreated into the ideological bunkers of despair, despondency, and defeatism. Many simply curled up and awaited the end.

But then, a voice was heard as one crying in the wilderness. "Arise! Shine! This is the United States of America. We deserve better than this; we are better than this; and we owe better than this to our children and to the world."

Ancient truths – long buried – were unearthed and unleashed. The Spirit of 1776 was rekindled. A tiny flame grew great and began to spread across the land. A mighty conflagration had been ignited, and from the rising smoke the clouds of war converged. On the one side a growing army of eagles assembled – proud, noble, brave, and true. They had gathered to save the life of their nation. Against them was formed a swarm of vultures. They had gathered to end the life of the nation so they could pick clean its bones. The die was cast. This would be war. This would be the Second American Revolution! AR2!

The first shot was fired in California. A new man arose from the ashes. He did not bow before the idol of the elephant nor the jack ass. His commitment was to principles, not politics. He swore to serve the people, not the party machines. He offered a plan that was unique. This was not merely a different shade of red or blue. This was exceptional, extraordinary. It was heroic, and it would prove to be historic. The machines tried to ignore him, but the people didn't. They began to listen, and the machines began to worry. The machinists argued, "He can't win. He isn't one of us! You're just throwing away your vote if you choose him." He countered, "They are the ones who created this mess, and yet they offer nothing to fix it. Aren't you just throwing away your vote if you choose one of them?" The people knew that he was right. They knew that if you do not vote your principles, you will lose even if your candidate does win the election. The machines were powerless to stop the might of the new, old ideas. Had they any integrity, the machinists would have conceded and joined the Revolution; but they had no integrity. For them politics and government weren't about the welfare of the people; it was about the welfare of the politicians. Their quiver was empty, save one, last arrow – slander. They drew the bolt, strung it, and let it fly.

The vultures unleashed all manner of vile accusations against this new man. They attacked him personally. They misrepresented his views. They sought to pit American against American in a time-tested campaign of divide and conquer. It worked with some; but other citizens came to realize that the ones the party politicians were trying to divide and conquer were all Americans. They asked, "Instead of trying to divide and conquer us, shouldn't they be trying to unite and empower us?"

The battle raged. Both sides understood what was at stake. Behind closed doors the leaders of the two party machines collaborated. They agreed, "We can't allow this S.O.B to win. We've got a good thing goin' for us. He could ruin it all." The machines secretly combined forces to combat the new man. The vultures counterattacked. Their war chests were expended to abort the rebirth of the True America. The eagles reeled backward – stunned and bloodied – from the fury of the blow. Hope flickered as it began to look as though the armies of darkness would again prevail.

But then, something unexpected happened. Eagles from coast to coast heard the battle cry of their brothers and sisters in the West. That cry was true and pure, but desperate. They realized that this fight was not for one state but for one nation under God! This was it. Do or die. Liberty or death! And from the farthest expanses of the land, the patriot flock gathered and raced to the aid of their comrades, talons unsheathed.

And then, something even more unexpected took place. The forces of righteousness – long dormant – began to stir and entered the fray. The community of faith found a new boldness and finally arose to combat the forces of darkness. A legion of white eagles assembled, soared, and then dove into battle, coming to the aid of their wounded and weary brethren. The vultures could not stand against the united power of the eagles. They never could. They never will. Now stunned and bloodied themselves, the vultures retreated into the darkness – not in defeat, but merely to await a more opportune time. In the end, the eagles prevailed. The new man was elected. But even greater travails awaited.

"In the Name of the Father and of the Son and of the Holy Spirit. Amen." The new man is inaugurated. He begins by consecrating his life, his administration, and his state to God almighty – just as did his forefather, George

Washington. And just as did George Washington, the new governor concludes his inaugural ceremony by going to worship at a nearby church. Eagles rejoice, but the vultures are already scheming to thwart the Revolution and its first general.

The Constitutional Governor strings his bow, draws his first arrow, aims, and lets it fly. Abortion – the supreme offense against both life and the right to it – is declared unconstitutional. The Governor orders all abortion clinics to close and all hospitals to cease all procedures except those absolutely necessary to save the life of the mother. He also declares an end to same-sex "marriage." Since rights are endowed by God then, clearly, anything outside the will of God cannot be a right. The judgment of Scripture is clear and undivided: homosexual conduct is an abomination. There is no right to it.

Second Amendment rights, long a target of the vultures, were immediately reestablished. The Governor ordered a blanket pardon for any and all individuals, businesses, and organizations convicted of violating the state's many anti-gun rights laws.

The Governor let fly a barrage of arrows all targeting the repressive legislation instituted by past assemblies of vultures in the state's capitol. Through payroll and compensation reform the people were given back control over the money they earned. Bosses, unions, and the government lost control of the strings they had used to reduce the working population to puppets. Income surged, pensions were saved, and freedom spread.

Through regulatory reform businesses were liberated from the straightjackets that had been crafted for them by the vultures. Productivity and employment soared. The power and oppression of government bureaucracies were slashed by an immediate 10% cut in their budgets with more to come. Additionally, the bureaucrats were rewarded for cutting costs and increasing efficiency. As a consequence, the rate at which the government shrunk was accelerated.

And then the Governor took dead-aim at the vampire sucking the life blood from a free and prosperous America. He declared the obvious: that it is clearly unconstitutional to take one person's property in order to redistribute it to another. Not one penny of tax dollars would be spent on "welfare", "entitlements", or other redistribution schemes. From now on, charity will be administered by charities; thereby eliminating government coercion and insuring a perfect coincidence between the free will of the contributor and the size and purpose of the contribution. No more will we allow the government to steal one person's earnings in order to buy the vote of another. The tax burden of the citizenry plummeted.

The liberty-lovers and productives rejoiced as they could already perceive the glow on the horizon heralding the dawn of a new day and the rebirth of America the Great. The vultures, however, saw things differently. They perceived the loss of everything for which they had labored for well over a century. This was do or die for them as well. They had to stop the Governor.

The vultures gathered to conspire in the dark, musty caves of Cartel boardrooms. A call went out to other vultures and their allies across the nation and, indeed, around the world. "Help us stop the Governor, or all will be lost!" Serpents from around the globe conspired with the vultures to prepare the counterattack. Billions of dollars were provided to fund the effort while puppet organizations were mobilized to begin the assault. As always, the poor and naive would be the shock troops. The vultures always found it easy to shed the blood and spend the lives of the very people they claimed to support.

"The Governor wants to take away your rights and your benefits!", shouted the vultures and their lackeys. "Fight back!" The elements of the population devoted to sloth and self-centered, other-destructive conveniences were rallied. They took to the streets. They occupied the parks. They converged on the state capitol. Meanwhile, other vulture organizations ostensibly dedicated to the empty euphemisms of "civil liberties" and "social justice" filed law suits, organized rallies at colleges and universities, and tapped their fellow travelers in the media to stop the Governor.

But the Governor would not yield. This would prove to be his greatest strength and something the enemy could not comprehend. You see, vultures and serpents expect everyone to be like them – self-seeking compromisers and turncoats. They are completely at a loss as to how to deal with a man of principle who would rather spend his life than compromise it. It took weeks, but the protesters tired and returned to their holes.

The "civil liberties" and "social justice" organizations easily won victories in the courts which they dominated, but the Governor thwarted them with a single word, "No!" He would not concede to the dictates of the traitorous justices who betrayed their oath to preserve, protect, and defend the Constitution. He had taken the same oath, but unlike them, he intended to keep it.

Now the vultures in the federal government took flight. They threatened the Governor with contempt and arrest. This time the Governor countered with two words, "Bring it!" The federal vultures balked. You see, while the protesters were protesting and the lawyers were lawyering, the eagles also were at work. The Constitutional Sheriffs were scrubbing clean their counties from the unconstitutional filth and grime that had built up over the decades. But they did something else as well. They formed and trained massive posses to aid in the defense of the Revolution. When the protesters crossed the line into violent and destructive behavior, the posse was called out to "convince" them to settle down – and they did. And when the federal vultures threatened to seize the Governor, the Constitutional Sheriffs and their posses surrounded him with a ring of steel. "You want him, you're gonna have to come through us."

The feds reconsidered, but they did not surrender. They tried another tactic. For decades the federal vultures had diligently insinuated themselves into nearly every aspect of public life at the state, county, and city level. They did this by promising funding for local projects, if the local government would simply accept a few, "reasonable" conditions. The lure of free money was more than most politicians could resist, and so a deal was struck. Once these lower governments developed a taste for federal loot, they became increasingly dependent upon it. This, in turn, gave the federal government frightful influence and power. The puppeteer's strings had been secured, and the puppet could now be jerked in any direction the puppet master directed. It now was time to play the money card against the Governor.

"If you do not accede to our demands", the federal vultures thundered, "we will cut off the billions of dollars you receive from the federal government."

"Fine", replied the Governor calmly. "If you discontinue federal funds to the people of my state, then the people of my state will discontinue paying taxes to the federal government. And if you think you are going to come here and collect them by force, then you can take it up with my posses."

The world watched. The feds blinked. They had no idea how to deal with such righteous resolve.

Meanwhile, life in the First State began to blossom. They had withstood the assault of the vultures and now were beginning to enjoy the fruits of their faithfulness.

Workers saw huge increases in income. Their take-home pay surged, they paid substantially less in taxes, and they acquired complete freedom as to how their earnings should be invested and spent. Productivity soared and employment exploded as the business environment flourished. Parents regained the freedom to raise their children according to their wisdom instead of the state's agenda. The schools were purged of immoral influences. Voluntary prayer was permitted, morals were taught, violence dropped, grades soared. Faith-based communities bloomed. The spirit of love and compassion sprouted anew, and since people had far more money at their disposal, charities were awash in new contributions. As a consequence, the truly needy found themselves far better off than in the dark days when they were dependent upon the vagaries of government programs.

Yet not all appreciated the reforms of the Revolution. The freeloaders had been cut off. Some of the more honorable among them went to work and shared in the blessings of the American way. Many others, however, sought to continue their profligate life styles. Since the First State would no longer coddle them, they packed and went elsewhere. And since these shirkers also were responsible for much of the crime and other woes in their communities, life in the First State became much safer for all.

A new sun had dawned in the west. It's light spread far, wide, and fast. Although the vulture-controlled media tried to spin the true story of the Revolution into a tale of greed, inequity, racism, and failure; they failed. Light travels faster than dark, and truth is more durable than lies. The Light and Truth of the Revolution became known across the land.

People and businesses in the other states saw what was happening in the First State and craved these blessings for themselves. When their local vultures resisted, these people and businesses began to pack up and head for a better life in the New America's first outpost. Furthermore, when many of the unproductives began deserting the First State for the more abundant troughs available in other places, those states found themselves in quite a quandary. The demand for government-provided services increased while the number of productives who provide the tax base for funding them decreased. A new dynamic had entered the political formula. If you did not become like the First State, you would suffer the loss of your productive assets, the erosion of your tax base, an increased demand for government services, and the growth of either your taxes or your deficit in order to fund these services – which, of course, only worked to drive out even more of your most productive assets.

Before long a Second State joined the Revolution. Then came a third, a tenth, and a thirtieth. The last holdouts of the old, repressive system quickly approached crush-depth. They were overwhelmed by the influx of unproductives and the exodus of their last, remaining asset-producers. Their choice was simple: you either surf this tsunami or you will be swamped by it. Join the Revolution or die! The remaining handful of holdouts collapsed, and new, Revolutionary leadership took over. In less time than it took to win the First American Revolution, the Second had prevailed.

Even before the final victories had been secured among all the states, the Revolutionaries began sending representatives to Washington, D. C. The Congress and White House were captured. The swords of the vanquished were surrendered and beaten into plowshares. God was returned to the throne and, once again, the Heaven-rescued land praised the power that hath made and preserved it a nation. America had blessed God, and so, God blessed America.

The Constitution was resurrected and reestablished as the secular authority of the nation. Schools everywhere again taught the noble truth of our past and insured that all future generations would read the Constitution through the lenses of the Declaration in order to secure the blessings of liberty to ourselves and our posterity.

The light of liberty shone brightly once again. But light makes shadows. The vultures and serpents had been vanquished but not exterminated. Their vile species retreated into the shadows, hiding until the next time the people took for granted their God-given rights and forgot the dedication and sacrifice that are necessary to preserve them.

But for now, a great victory had been won; and a joyous celebration had begun. We were once again one nation under God. We were once again, America the Great! And each generation of American would turn to the next and declare, "Here is the blessing of Heaven, if you can keep it."

A R 2

The power. The glory.

Amen.

JOIN THE REVOLUTION!

"These are the times that try men's souls: The summer soldier and the sunshine patriot will, in this crisis, shrink from the service of his country; but he that stands by it now, deserves the love and thanks of man and woman."

Thomas Paine's pamphlet, *The American Crisis*, opened with these words. These are the words that General George Washington had read to his battered and bloodied army on December 23, 1776. The fate of the United States, a scant five months old, teetered perilously on the brink of catastrophe. The Continental Army had been relentlessly beaten back by the British since the previous summer. Disaster seemed imminent. Washington issued a call to arms as if to say, "Show your colors, America. Show your colors!" We answered the call. We bled red leaving a scarlet track in the pure, white snow to lead the way for others. We proved true blue to the cause of liberty and for our posterity. Three days later the battered and beaten arose to batter and beat the enemy at Trenton. Scarcely a week after that, on January 3, the Americans struck again, vanquishing the British at Princeton. The young nation was spared, and the Revolution continued.

These are, once again, the times that try men's souls; once again Americans are called to show your colors; and once again those who stand by the cause of liberty deserve the love and thanks of man and woman, today and tomorrow.

Answer the call. Spread the word.

Just as Paul Revere sounded the alarm and spread the word to protect his countrymen against the tyranny of the British Monarchy in 1775, you can spread the word to protect and unite your countrymen against the tyranny that oppresses us today.

Take advantage of our bulk rates and give copies of ***AR2: Handbook for the Second American Revolution*** to friends, family, neighbors, school teachers, pastors, libraries, and community leaders. Distribute them through your veteran and patriot organizations, churches, Chambers of Commerce, and other groups.

<u>EDUCATE AND LEGISLATE</u>. Give a copy to your elected officials and candidates for office. Tell them you will not vote for them unless they publicly proclaim to support and defend the cause of ***AR2.***

Call (909) 913-7878 to get a quote for volume discounts and shipping costs.

MEET THE AUTHOR

Invite Lawrence Paul Hebron to talk with your organization about
joining the Revolution, resurrecting the Constitution,
and rebuilding America the Great.
Call (909) 913-7878 for details.
See our website: www.AR2thebook.com

AND FOR STILL MORE

ADD TO YOUR COLLECTION OF REVOLUTIONARY IDEAS.
Be sure to read
***Solutions: Guidebook for Rebuilding
America the Great***
by
Lawrence Paul Hebron

UNCHAIN THE AMERICAN EAGLE!
The dream of July 4, 1776, has become the
nightmare of today.
The "usual suspects" of American politics offer nothing
new – just more of the same bad medicine that made
us sick in the first place.

WE DESERVE BETTER!
HERE IT IS.

This is a worker's guide – a handbook to fix America.

The problem of big government – SOLVED!

The problem of government deficits – SOLVED!

The problem of keeping government under control
– SOLVED!

The problem of protecting your wages from government theft – SOLVED!

The problem of illegal drugs – SOLVED!

The problem of illegal immigrants – SOLVED!

The problem of bad parenting and bad schooling
– SOLVED!

Restoring the missing "X" Factor that politicians won't
talk about – SOLVED!

Hang on – this won' be pretty!

This is a no-nonsense, take-no-prisoners

GUIDEBOOK FOR REBUILDING AMERICA THE GREAT.

Only the bold should proceed.

For more information see

www.solutionsthebook.com

To order from Amazon, go to

www.amazon.com

then search under "Lawrence Paul Hebron."

9521833R00142

Made in the USA
San Bernardino, CA
20 March 2014